THE
FAMILY
CREATIVE
WORKSHOP

Enamelling Metal, Fantasy
Flowers, Framing, Fur Re-cycling,
Gingerbread, Glass Working, Gold Leafing,
Granny Squares, Hammocks and Slings,
Hardanger Embroidery, Heraldry, Herbs

Plenary Publications International

The Project-Evaluation Symbols appearing in the title heading at the beginning of each project have these meanings:

Estimated time to completion for an unskilled adult:

 Hours

 Days

 Weeks

Suggested level of experience:

 Child alone

 Supervised child or family project

 Unskilled adult

 Specialized prior training

Tools and equipment:

 Small hand tools

 Large hand and household tools

 Specialized or powered equipment

Publishers
Plenary Publications International, Incorporated, New York.

For this volume
Contributing editors: Sally Foy, Anne Masters, Douglas Whitworth.

Acknowledgements:
Page 51—Egyptian vase, courtesy Corning Museum of Glass, New York; page 113—courtesy Local History and Genealogy Division, New York Public Library, Astor, Lenox and Tilden Foundation; pages 110, 112—artwork courtesy Van Nostrand Reinhold © 1969.

On the cover
Tissue and crepe paper sheets, cut, folded, fluffed and tipped with a felt pen. See the entry Fantasy Flowers, beginning on page 14. Photograph by Paul Levin.

ISBN 0 7054 0335 1

Filmsetting by C. E. Dawkins (Typesetters) Ltd., London, SE1 1UN.
Printed in Holland by Smeets Lithographers, Weert.
Bound by Proost en Brandt N.V., Amsterdam.

METRIC CONVERSION CHART

EXACT CONVERSIONS: METRIC TO IMPERIAL

1 gramme = 0.035 ounces
1 kilogramme = 2.205 pounds
1 millimetre = 0.039 inches
1 centimetre = 0.394 inches

1 metre = 1.094 yards
1 millilitre = 0.035 fluid ounces
1 litre = 1.76 pints
1 litre = 0.22 gallons

OUNCES TO GRAMMES

oz	g	oz	g
1/2	14	7	198
3/4	21	8	226
1	28	9	255
1 1/2	42	10	283
1 3/4	50	11	311
2	56	12	340
3	85	13	368
4	113	14	396
5	141	15	425
6	170	16	453

POUNDS TO KILOGRAMMES

lb	kg	lb	kg
1	0.5	11	5.0
2	0.9	12	5.6
3	1.4	13	5.9
4	1.8	14	6.3
5	2.3	15	6.8
6	2.7	16	7.3
7	3.2	17	7.7
8	3.6	18	8.2
9	4.0	19	8.6
10	4.5	20	9.0

INCHES TO MILLIMETRES

in	mm
1/8	3
1/4	6
3/8	10
1/2	13
5/8	15
3/4	20
7/8	22
1	25
2	50
3	75

INCHES TO CENTIMETRES

in	cm	in	cm
1	2.5	11	28.0
2	5.0	12	30.5
3	7.5	13	33.0
4	10.0	14	35.5
5	12.5	15	38.0
6	15.0	16	40.5
7	18.0	17	43.0
8	20.5	18	46.0
9	23.0	19	48.5
10	25.5	20	51.0

YARDS TO METRES

yd	m
1/8	0.15
1/4	0.25
3/8	0.35
1/2	0.50
5/8	0.60
3/4	0.70
7/8	0.80
1	0.95
2	1.85
3	2.75

FLUID OUNCES TO MILLILITRES

fl oz	ml	fl oz	ml
1	28	11	312
2	57	12	341
3	85	13	369
4	114	14	398
5	142	15	426
6	171	16	454
7	200	17	483
8	227	18	511
9	256	19	540
10	284	20	568

PINTS TO LITRES

pt	lit
1/4	0.1
1/2	0.3
1	0.5
2	1.0
3	1.7
4	2.3
5	2.8
6	3.4
7	4.0
8	4.5

GALLONS TO LITRES

gall	lit
1	4.5
2	9.0
3	13.6
4	18.2
5	22.7
6	27.3
7	31.8
8	36.4
9	41.0
10	45.5

(All figures have been rounded off to simplify the tables.)

Contents

Enamelling Metal 6
By Ellen Green.
PROJECTS: Copper pendant; copper dish. *Craftnotes*: Firing Safety.

Fantasy Flowers 14
By Marilyn Nierenberg; Carl Caronia.
PROJECTS: Pencil posy; tissue paper blossoms; foil flowers; sculpted roses and tulips; feather duster centrepieces; fabric flowers.

Framing 24
By Beth Wigren.
PROJECTS: Basic wood moulding frame; metal frame; stick frame; background frame; box frame.

Fur Re-cycling 32
By Lee K. Thorpe.
PROJECTS: Making a fur pillow; shortening a fur coat; designing and making a fur collar and cuffs; fashioning a stole. *Craftnote*: Sewing fur, fur care.

Gingerbread 42
By Albert Hadener; Lisa Bosboom.
PROJECTS: Fairy-tale house; gingerbread biscuits. *Craftnotes*: Enlarging patterns.

Glass Working 50
By Carl H. Betz; Suellen Fowler.
PROJECTS: Lead glass beads; swizzle sticks; form-a-loop sculpture; lampblown glass bottle; blown glass beads; blown glass ornament. *Craftnotes*: Making coloured glass rods.

Gold Leafing 64
By Walter Methner.
PROJECTS: Gilt-edge shadow box; gold leafing a carved chair; applying gold to glassware; lettering a sign in gold.

Granny Squares 74
By Connie Kuznekoff.
PROJECTS: Traditional granny-square afghan; place mat; floral granny-square afghan; cap-and-scarf set; popcorn granny-square afghan; shoulder tote bag. *Craftnotes*: Blocking; joining squares.

Hammocks and Slings 86
By Joe Scheurer.
PROJECTS: Canvas log tote or sling; naval hammock. *Craftnotes*: Hammocks and slings.

Hardanger Embroidery 94
By Marion Scoular; Rita Allgood Tubbs.
PROJECTS: Bookmark; cocktail mat; wine place mat and napkin; white place mat and napkin. *Craftnotes*: Stitches.

Heraldry 106
By William Metzig; J. P. Brooke-Little.
PROJECT: Designing your own coat of arms.

Herbs 116
By Mrs. A. DeCiantis; Marilyn Ratner.
PROJECTS: Hanging garden; harvesting and drying herbs; gift-basket garden starter; herb note cards; recipes.

ENAMELLING METAL
Fusing Colour in a Kiln

By Ellen Green

Enamel is an enduring, lustrous, coloured glaze on a metal base. The enameller creates the glaze by applying glass—usually as a powder but sometimes in other forms such as lumps or threads or even moist dabs—to a clean metal surface, and heating the piece in a kiln. The heat of the kiln melts the glass and fuses it to the metal in a smooth even coat.

Ear-rings, bracelets, pendants and other small articles of jewellery require only a small kiln. Instructions for making a pendant, in which small dabs of enamel melt into a flower-like design, begin on page 9. These instructions also include directions for the three basic operations of all enamelling: cleaning the surface of the metal, applying the enamel, and firing in a kiln.

The shallow dish shown in the photograph on page 13 requires a larger kiln. Its design was created by sifting powdered enamel of different colours through a strainer on to the surface of a pre-formed piece of copper. Instructions for making a similar dish start on page 12.

How enamel is made

The term "enamel" can be confusing. To a handyman it may refer to a hard, glossy paint used on woodwork and metal. To a dentist, it is the coating on a tooth. But to an artist, true enamel is a thin layer of glass fused to a metal surface. The colours can be vivid or subdued, the design bold or subtle, or as plain as the working surface of an enamelled kitchen stove or other household appliance.

The basis of enamel is flux, a clear glass compound of silica with other minerals that keep its melting point fairly low—around 820° C—and make it lustrous. The flux is coloured by the addition of metal oxides while it is molten. Cobalt oxide, for example, turns the flux blue. Iron oxide creates red or brown. Copper oxide makes green. The character of the additive also determines whether the enamel is opaque, translucent or, as can happen in a few cases, opalescent.

When the molten glass cools, it is broken into chunks and ground to powder or made into other forms for use by the enameller.

Start with eight or 10 colours of 80-mesh enamel. It comes in a great variety of colours and you can experiment as you go along. If you want to keep using a colour, record its number. Manufacturers change the names of colours frequently, but the numbers remain the same. Other materials you will need include an enamel adhesive, a liquid that holds the enamel powder to the surface of the metal, such as gum tramil; a copper cleaning solution; fine steel wool; waxed paper and heavy glazed paper.

Metals to enamel

Copper is the metal most widely used for enamelling; it forms a bond readily with molten glass and it can withstand as many as 10 firings in a kiln without deteriorating. You can purchase pre-formed copper shapes such as the ones used here for the pendant and the shallow dish. Craft supply shops carry a great variety of copper articles, from small pieces for jewellery to bowls, dishes and boxes, as well as the fittings necessary for mounting jewellery.

Powdered enamels of various shades, translucent and opaque, are fired on copper discs to produce brilliant glossy colours. For extra effect use millefiore—chips of patterned glass rod (available in enamelling craft shops) as seen in the centre of the picture opposite. Arrange them, patterned face upwards, on discs which have already been counter-enamelled (see page 10). Fire the discs a second time until the millefiore pattern has melted and spread out.

Enamelling gold or silver produces striking results, but enamellers rarely attempt it until they are skilled. The high cost of these metals makes mistakes very expensive.

Enamelling equipment

The enameller's most important piece of equipment is the kiln. This is the insulated, electrically heated oven where crushed silica glass particles are fused on to a metal base, resulting in a smooth, brilliant coat. Kilns vary in size and cost from about £10 to £100. Pyrometers, which measure high temperatures and heat controls, are optional.

Match your firing equipment to the size of your kiln. This equipment should include at least two asbestos boards—one to put the kiln on, and one to hold hot tools and work that has been removed from the kiln to cool—as well as a steel firing mesh, sometimes called a planche (pictured on opposite page), which serves as a convenient platform for small objects; assorted firing stilts (also pictured opposite); tongs or large tweezers; and an enamelling spatula or enamelling fork. Asbestos gloves are recommended for handling enamelling equipment in the kiln, especially for large items. These should be worn throughout firing to handle hot equipment and to remove the piece as soon as it is ready. Substitutes for asbestos gloves, such as oven gloves or pot holders, should not be used since they are not sufficiently heat-resistant for the high temperatures involved in enamelling.

Other equipment you will need: an 80-mesh enamelling strainer; round and flat brushes; an atomizer; small paper or plastic cups; a very small spatula for manipulating small quantities of enamel; a replaceable-blade knife; a large plastic bowl; a rubber kitchen spatula; a carborundum stone.

Enamelling equipment and materials are usually available at craft shops, but it may be easier to order by mail. Crafts Unlimited, at 178 Kensington High Street, London W.8, have a good range of enamelling materials.

CRAFTNOTES: FIRING SAFETY

Enamelling is no more dangerous than cooking or carpentry, but like these activities, it demands safe working habits.

Kilns rarely overheat, but they can. The safest practice is to remain in the room while a kiln is turned on. An unattended kiln can be a danger to others—small children, particularly.

Always wear asbestos gloves while firing. The 820°C. temperature of the kiln can heat the spatula or enamelling fork in your hand very quickly. Keep the gloves on throughout the firing; the time is short and you will be prepared to remove a piece the instant it is ready.

Arrange your work area so that you can move a piece from the kiln to the asbestos board where it will cool, without having to lift it over or around any obstruction.

Make sure the cooling board is in a place where you will not be likely to brush inadvertently against a hot piece of enamel while you are at work on something else.

Never leave hot work unattended. It does not look hot and someone might attempt to pick it up. A severe burn would result.

Stand, rather than sit, while firing. If a hot piece of work does tumble from the spatula, it will be easier to get out of the way if you are on your feet than if you are seated.

Store inflammable liquids in another room. A hot kiln can ignite vapours from paints, lacquers, solvents and similar materials.

Always work in a well-ventilated room, but do not place your kiln or cooling board in a direct draught. Sudden changes in temperature can crack an enamel surface before it is cool.

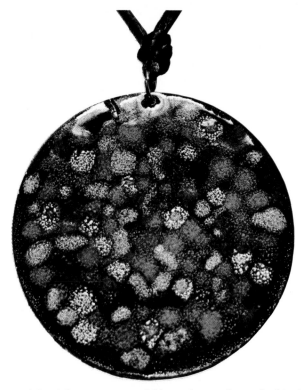

Dabs of enamel created the elaborate pattern of this pendant as they melted in the kiln.

Jewellery, Lapidary and Metalwork
Copper Pendant

The pendant shown in the photograph above can be fired in a small kiln. See page 8 for basic enamelling equipment and materials for this project. You will also need a 7.5 cm disc of 18-gauge copper with a small hole drilled near the edge; a neck cord for the pendant and a split ring to join pendant and cord.

Getting ready
Turn on your kiln to heat. Spread waxed paper on your enamelling table. Put a planche on the paper and a small enamelling stilt on the planche.

Mix a solution of copper cleaner and water in a plastic bowl, stirring with a rubber spatula. Non-metallic materials must be used for this because metal could react with the cleaner and subsequently with the copper. If you do not want to use a commercial preparation, make your own by dissolving $1\frac{1}{2}$ table-spoons of salt in 250 ml of vinegar.

Cleaning the copper
The copper disc must be absolutely clean. Grease and dirt can create dark spots under the enamel and even prevent the enamel from adhering to the copper. Clean the disc by heating it in the kiln, cooling it and soaking it in the cleaner.

Look in your kiln. If the interior glows cherry red it is hot enough for enamelling. If you have a kiln with a pyrometer to measure high temperatures, the instrument should indicate 750-800° C. Put on asbestos gloves and place the disc into the kiln with an enamelling spatula. Leave it there until it glows red. Then lift it out with the spatula and put it on the asbestos board to cool.

As soon as the disc is cool enough to touch, pick it up with tweezers (photograph 1) and rub each side with fine steel wool. Rinse the disc under running water to remove any cleaning solution or steel wool splinters, then dry it with paper towels, holding the disc through the paper, so that your hands do not touch the copper. Place the disc on the enamelling stilt.

1: Remove the copper disc from the cleaning solution with tweezers. Oil or grease on the surface—even fingerprints—can flaw the enamel.

2: Place the disc on an enamelling stilt until you are ready to spray it with binder. The stilt is on a steel mesh sometimes called a planche.

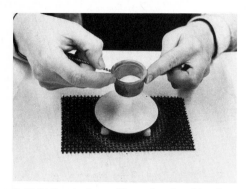

3: Hold the strainer with one hand and tap it with the forefinger of the other hand to sift enamel on to the disc. Do edge first, then centre.

4: Dry the piece on top of the kiln. If you use a large kiln, hold the piece inside it on a spatula for 3 seconds, then remove it.

5: Lift work into the kiln with a spatula. This table is heat proof. If you enamel at home put kiln on an asbestos board. Keep another board handy for hot work and tools.

Laying the foundation

The disc must have an unflawed layer of enamel on each side. The layer on the front acts as a base for dabs of enamel that form the design. The layer on the back is to prevent the piece from warping. It is called counter-enamel. Every flat or nearly flat piece of enamel work is counter-enamelled so that, when the piece shrinks as it cools, the stresses on the back and front are equal.

Make sure your hands are clean. If you are using a vinegar and salt solution, dip your fingertips in it and dry them on a paper towel. Pick up the disc with your fingertips just touching the edge. Do not let them curl over and touch the surface. Hold the disc vertically and spray one face with enamel binder, an adhesive that holds enamel powder to metal. Hold the atomizer about 45 cm from the disc and cover it with an even coat without drips or runs. Return the disc to the stilt with the sprayed side up.

Sifting powder on the disc

Fill an 80-mesh enamelling strainer with green 80-mesh enamel. Hold the strainer full of enamel with one hand and tap it gently with the forefinger of the other as you move the strainer over the disc, first around the rim and then over the centre (photograph 3). Let the enamel fall from the strainer so that it forms a smooth layer on the disc, somewhat thicker around the edge.

Make sure no copper shows through the powder, but keep the thickness of the layer less than the thickness of the copper. If the enamel is too thin, it will burn off when you fire it. If it is too thick, it will crack when it cools. Spray the dusted surface with binder, holding the atomizer far enough away for the mist to fall on the enamel powder without disturbing it.

After you have sprayed the enamelled surface with binder, return the disc to the stilt with the bare copper side up and the side with the enamel powder on it down. The binder will prevent the powder from falling off. Sift enamel over the bare surface, just as you did for the reverse side. You do not need to apply binder this time because you will not turn the piece over again before it is fired. After the enamel is applied, if the hole is clogged with powder, clean it with a toothpick.

Do not worry about wasting the enamel that misses the disc. The paper beneath the planche will catch it. When you have finished sifting enamel, gather the fallen powder in the paper and pour it back into its container. If you have applied several colours at once and there is a mixture on the paper, keep it in a separate container. You can use this for counter-enamelling.

The first firing

When the enamel powder is moist with binder or water, it must be dried before firing or the moisture will turn to steam when the piece is in the kiln. Steam bubbles trapped in the molten enamel will pit and crack the surface.

If you are using a small kiln, simply pick up the whole stack—planche, stilt and disc—and place it on top of the kiln, where the warmth will evaporate the moisture in 4 or 5 minutes (photograph 4). Then, put on asbestos gloves, place the stack on the enamelling spatula and put it in the kiln (photograph 5).

You can also combine drying with firing. Wear asbestos gloves. Slide the blade of the enamelling spatula under the planche—the whole stack is always put into the kiln or removed as a unit—and hold the stack in the kiln for 3 seconds. This is long enough to evaporate the moisture, but not long enough to melt the enamel. Hold the work outside the kiln for 5 or 6 seconds to let all the moisture escape, then return it to the kiln and close the door or lid.

When enamel is fired, it first turns dark. Then the surface turns grainy as the particles of enamel melt and coagulate. Finally, after about 3 minutes, the surface appears smooth and glossy. When this occurs the piece is fired.

Watch the disc in the kiln and remove it before it reaches the final stage of firing. The surface should still be grainy. It will become smooth in later firings. Use the enamelling spatula to transfer it from the kiln to the asbestos cooling board. As the piece cools, its colour will change from very dark to the colour of the finished enamel.

Correcting flaws

When the piece is cool inspect it. If there are small cracks, do not worry. These will close up during subsequent firings. If the enamel is burned away, there is little you can do, although you might clean it, dry it, dust it with clear flux and fire it. Sometimes overfiring produces interesting patterns.

The most likely flaws will show around the rim, where the enamel has crept away from the edge, or in the centre where tiny specks of copper may be visible through a thin coat of enamel.

Use a camel's hair brush to paint any bare spots at the edge with binder, then counter-enamel and enamel the piece again, as you did the first time. This second coat of enamel is applied to both sides whether there are flaws or not.

Applying the design

While the work is cooling, prepare moist enamel. You need six or eight small non-metallic cups, one for each colour of the design. I use disposable plastic drinking cups with the tops cut off.

Place a small amount of enamel in each cup and add enough water to wet the enamel without leaving any free water in it. The consistency of beach sand when it is cohesive enough for building sand castles is just right. One way to achieve the right consistency is to tilt the cup so that the water and enamel are at one side, then tilt the cup in the opposite direction and let the water run out, leaving a damp heap of enamel at one side of the cup.

6: Apply more dabs of moist enamel with a spatula, as shown here, after the first application of dabs has been fired, or use a toothpick or the wooden end of a kitchen match.

7: After the final firing of the pendant, rub heat-blackened copper from the edge of the disc with a carborundum stone. Keep both stone and pendant wet while you do this.

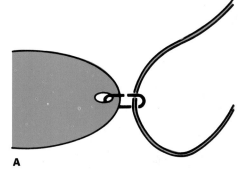

A

Figure A: A small split ring links pendant and neck cord. The ring, cord and a large variety of other jewellery fittings for enamelled work are available at craft supply shops.

Pick up dabs of moist enamel with a very small spatula, a toothpick or the wooden end of a kitchen match, and cover the disc with dots of different coloured enamels, creating a design as you go along.

When the disc is filled with enamel dabs, dry and fire it. This time leave it in the kiln until the surface is smooth and glossy. The dabs may appear as slight lumps, but the overall surface should be smooth. In all subsequent firings leave the piece in the kiln for a complete firing like this one.

Let the piece cool on the asbestos board, apply more dabs of enamel to round out the design (photograph 6). Dry it, fire it and cool it, then sift a light coat of a translucent enamel on the surface. This should be just a dusting. After the piece has been fired and cooled again, the lumps will have levelled off to a flat or nearly flat surface. Some of the edges will be blended while others will have kept their sharpness. Some of the enamel will have broken into flecks of one colour within another colour. You can create more blends and flecks by dusting the piece lightly with flux and firing it again.

After the disc has finally cooled, clean the blackened edge with a carborundum stone. Keep the disc and stone wet in a bowl of water (photograph 7) or under a running tap while you rub the edge down to bare copper.

When the edge is clean, pry open the split ring with a scissor blade and insert it in the hole in the pendant. Run neck cord through the ring and squeeze the split ring closed (Figure A). The pendant is complete.

Enamelled Dish

The design on the shallow dish shown in the photograph opposite was created with dry enamel powder sifted on the surface so that the colours overlapped at the edges.

You will need a pre-formed dish of 18-gauge copper, 15 cm square with rounded corners and slightly sloping sides. You will also need a larger kiln than the one used to make the pendant (page 9) and a larger enamelling stilt.

Clean the copper dish as you cleaned the pendant disc, spray the bottom side with enamel binder, and place the disc bottom up on the stilt (photograph 8). The stilt should be on a sheet of wax paper that will catch loose enamel, but no planche is necessary. As it is on short legs a firing tool can be slid beneath it.

For counter-enamelling, you can use a mixture of salvaged enamels or you can use the same colour you have selected as the background colour.

When you sift, hold the enamel strainer so the forefinger of the same hand is free to tap it. You will need the other hand to tilt the dish. As you sift enamel on each sloping side, raise the stilt beneath it slightly so the dish tilts enough to make the sloping edge horizontal, so that the enamel falls on a level surface.

Pick the dish up with your fingertips holding the edges, as you did the pendant, and spray the powdered surface with binder again. Turn it over and spray binder on the face of the dish, and place it on the stilt face up. Sift enamel on the face of the dish. As you cover each edge, level it by lifting gently on the opposite side.

The next step is to dry and fire the piece. Wear asbestos gloves. Slide an enamelling fork or spatula under the stilt. Hold the work in the kiln for 3 seconds (photograph 9), remove it long enough to allow the moisture of the binder to dissipate, and return it to the kiln. Fire the piece until the surface is grainy, then place it on an asbestos board. When the dish is cool, paint any bare spots at the edges with binder, counter-enamel and enamel again.

Applying the design
The colours of this design were sifted on to the piece dry, rather than applied in moist dabs as they were for the pendant. I used a very dark green, cocoa, brick, and a light red over a yellow background.

Using an 80-mesh strainer, sift the colours on the dish one at a time, lifting the stilt to level the edges as you cover them (photograph 10). Use fairly large masses, bands, curves or other elements, allowing the colours to overlap at the edges. You can also move enamel about on the surface with a brush.

Fire the piece until the surface is smooth and glossy. Let it cool and sift more colour as necessary. If you are satisfied stop; but if you want to continue, you can. I worked on the design through two firings, then sifted on a light coating of transparent orange enamel and fired again. To complete the dish, clean the blackened copper at its edge with the carborundum stone.

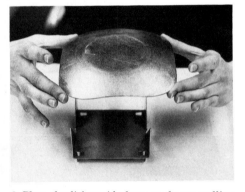

8: Place the dish upside down on the enamelling stilt after it has been cleaned and the bottom has been sprayed with binder. This large stilt requires no planche. Simply slide a fork or spatula underneath and lift.

9: Dry off the moisture in the binder by holding the piece in the kiln for 3 seconds. Remove it for 5 to 6 seconds to let the moisture evaporate, then return it to the kiln for firing.

10: Level a sloping edge by reaching under the piece with your fingers and raising the stilt to tilt the piece. It is easier to cover a level surface with powder than a sloping one.

11: You can use a brush to manipulate enamel powder on the surface. Here the powder is swept into a sharp edge. Other implements, such as a toothpick, create different effects.

The design on this shallow dish was created by sifting enamel powder
on to a pre-formed copper shape.

FANTASY FLOWERS
Beauty for all Seasons

By Marilyn Nierenberg

Artificial flowers can reflect the colours of spring throughout the year. Since no upkeep is required, they are easy to live with, and they make ideal get-well gifts, party displays, or decorations for your home.

Designs for artificial flowers can be adapted from nature or they can be your own inventions. One of the projects in this entry describes how crepe paper can be stretched and curled to resemble roses and tulips; another shows how sparkling metallic chrysanthemums and daisies are made from discarded pie pans; another is a gay bouquet from fabric matching your upholstery.

To design the pencil posy below, or any of the blossoms in this section, simply trace the parts of the pattern shown full size. As you outline the shapes, be sure to make a separate cardboard template for each part; dotted lines indicate cutting lines. To avoid destroying your book, place a sheet of carbon paper on top of a piece of thin cardboard and place them both beneath the pattern. Transfer each shape on to the cardboard by tracing over the pattern with a stylus (you can use the point of a dried-up ball point pen). Then, cut out the pattern which is now ready for use.

Toys and Games
Pencil Posy

This beginning project, the pencil posy, is an easy one for you and your child to assemble in a matter of minutes. You will need cardboard and scissors; and each posy will require at least two pieces of coloured felt 7 by 12 cm, a pencil with a rubber, and a bead threaded on a straight pin about 1 cm long.

Trace the patterns in Figure A on cardboard and cut out; then place the smallest and largest cardboard patterns on one scrap of felt and trace the outline on to the felt with a ballpoint pen. Trace the middle circle on to felt of a contrasting colour. Cut along dotted lines of the smallest circle to create petals for the posy.

To assemble the posy, stack the three felt pieces, aligning centres, with the smallest piece on top and the largest on the bottom. Run the pin with the bead on it through the felt and into the rubber.

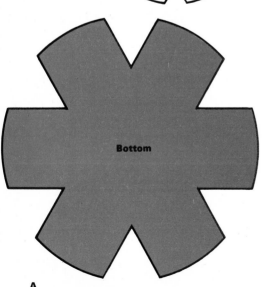

A

Figure A: For a pencil posy, top and bottom patterns are cut from one colour of felt, the middle pattern from a contrasting colour.

Want a neat, quick project to make with your child? Rubber-tipped pencils and crayons can be dressed up with colourful posies of soft felt fabric made from patterns shown on the left.

To form this attractive tissue paper bouquet, also shown on the cover, see Figures B to E, right.

Paper Folding and Cutting
Tissue Paper Flowers

The translucency of tissue paper can give flowers a luminous quality, yet the paper has sufficient body to be folded for making flowers. Craft or florist's shops stock the following materials that you will need: a selection of colourful tissue paper sheets 25 by 38 cm; one dozen stem wires 50 cm long; green floral tape for concealing the wire; a block of plastic foam cut to the diameter of your vase; and a pair of scissors.

To make one of the medium-sized flowers shown above, you will need six multi-coloured sheets of tissue paper about 25 by 38 cm. Stack the sheets evenly, then fold all six layers together in accordion pleats (as in Figure B). Each pleat should measure approximately 3 cm wide. Pinch the centre of the strip lengthways at the 12.5 cm midpoint, and wrap one end of a stem wire twice around the middle to hold the pleated paper in place. The shape should then roughly resemble a bow tie as in Figure C.

To make scalloped petals, cut a semi-circle at each end of the bow tie as shown on the left side in Figure C. Pointed petals are made by cutting triangles at both sides of the bow tie, as on the right side in Figure C. Or try designing your own petal cuts to shape the flower. After cutting petal shapes, cup both sides of the bow (see Figure D), and carefully fluff out the petals. Holding the floral tape in one hand, wind the tape around the wire stem in a spiral, working from just below the centre of the bow tie to the end of the wire (Figure E). Use a delicate touch to separate the layers of tissue paper and make the flower blossom. Place a plastic foam disc in the bottom of an empty coffee tin or tall vase suitable for the size of the flowers. If you use a coffee tin, cover it with coloured paper, hessian, or felt. After you have made enough flowers for your design, arrange them by poking their wire stems into the foam.

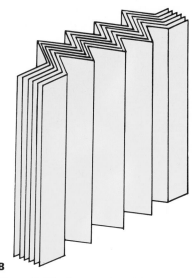

B

Figure B: The first step is to fold six stacked sheets of tissue into even accordion pleats.

C

Figure C: Shape ends of petals by making either semi-circular cuts (left) or pointed cuts (right) on both ends of the tissue paper "bow".

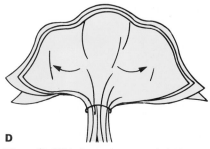

D

Figure D: With fingertips, stretch folds outwards to shape tissue paper into a bowl.

E

Figure E: Use a spiral motion to wrap the entire stem with self-sticking, green floral tape, working from bow to end of wire.

15

Paper Folding and Cutting
Foil Flowers

The stiff, self-supporting sheet aluminium used in foil pans and pie dishes can be cut and shaped into intricate flower-like forms. By following these patterns and instructions, you can transform foil into dazzling floral arrangements. Three 20 cm diameter aluminium pans will yield the 12 flowers shown in the bouquet on the opposite page. Coloured foil can also be used. One 4 m roll of aluminium wire for stems; a sheet of cooking foil 30 by 50 cm to cover stem wires; epoxy cement and long-nosed pliers are also needed.

Both daisies and chrysanthemums are made in essentially the same way, using three circles of aluminium. Figure F gives a full-sized pattern for the circle that forms the top layer of either flower. Figures G and H are patterns for the second and third layers of the daisy. Figures I and J are patterns for the second and third layers of the chrysanthemum. Figure K shows how the sections of each flower will be assembled later on a wire stem. Trace patterns on to tracing tissue and transfer them to thin cardboard with carbon paper. Cut out cardboard templates of top layer (Figure F) and petals (Figures G, H, I and J). Lay each pattern on the flat aluminium. With a pencil, outline patterns and cut out aluminium shapes along traced lines. To make the 16 segments shown in Figure F, place the cardboard circle over the aluminium circle and cut through both along the dotted lines. Punch a small hole in the centre of each aluminium shape with a scissor point. Cut a 25 cm length of wire to make a supporting stem for each flower.

Top

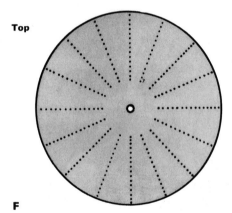

F

Figure F: Use this pattern for the top of each flower. Cut on dotted lines for curls.

Middle

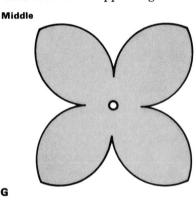

G

Figure G: Use this pattern for the middle layer of petals on a daisy.

Bottom

H

Figure H: Make the bottom layer of petals for a daisy from this pattern.

Middle

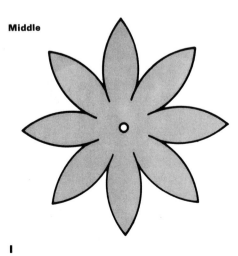

I

Figure I: Use this pattern for the middle layer of petals for a chrysanthemum.

Bottom

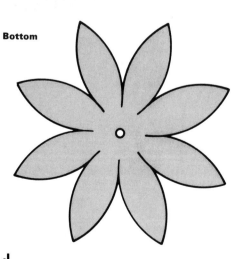

J

Figure J: Use this pattern to make the bottom layer of petals for a chrysanthemum.

K

Figure K: Middle and bottom layers of flower slide under top layer and are glued in place.

Shaping and assembling the daisy

Curl each segment of the top layer of the daisy upwards and inwards, using round-nose pliers as in photograph 1. To shape the petals of the middle and bottom layers, grip the centreline of each petal and bend upwards. Pinch both halves of each petal inwards with your fingers until they almost touch.

Make a small loop at the end of a stem wire by bending it around a pencil. Twist the ends together firmly. Slide the loop off the pencil and bend it at a right angle to the stem. Coat the underside of the loop with epoxy cement. Push the stem through the daisy top (Figure K, opposite) and pull it downwards until the cemented surface of the loop is pressed against centre of the foil. Ease the curled petals aside with your fingers to allow the loop to pass. Let the epoxy set. Then coat centre portions of the top side of the second layer with epoxy and slide it up on the stem until it touches the underside of the top layer. Repeat this procedure with bottom layer, adjusting it on the wire before gluing so that all petals show.

Shaping and assembling the chrysanthemum

Make the top layer of the chrysanthemum as you did the daisy, by curling the petals upwards. Alternate upward and downward curls for the middle layer (Figure I). Curve all segments of the bottom layer (Figure J) downwards.

Assemble and cement the chrysanthemums as you did the daisy, sliding first the top layer on to the stem, then the middle layer, and finally the bottom layer, with epoxy applied where all layers will touch.

Making and attaching the leaves

Long curling leaves can be cut from the crinkled sides of the foil pans (photograph 3). Make each leaf about 2.5 cm wide at its widest point, and about 7.5 cm long, but with an additional 5 mm by 2.5 cm strip at its base. This strip will be bound to the stem after the stem has been wrapped. To wrap the stem cut a strip of aluminium cooking foil 1 cm wide and 50 cm long. Begin wrapping the stem directly below the bottom layer of petals. No glue is required since the foil conforms to the shape of the wire. Press the foil firmly in place as you twirl the stem. Attach the leaves by twisting the 2.5 cm strip at their base around the middle of the stem and wrap cooking foil around the juncture of strip and stem to cover. For your floral arrangement, snip stems to various lengths and stick them into the plastic foam base or clay mound fitted into a vase or tin covered with decorative paper. Cover base with white pebbles.

1: Curl the petals in the top layer of each flower tightly with pliers. A curled top layer is shown on the left. Curl the middle and the bottom layers as indicated in text.

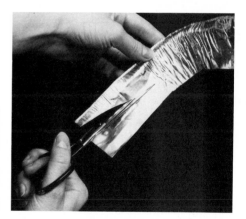

2: Bend the centre of each daisy petal upwards with pliers; push the petal inwards with fingertips. Complete petal is shown at right.

3: Cut long, curling leaves from the crinkled edges of pie pans. The text gives dimensions.

This cocktail table centrepiece started out as four aluminium foil pans.

Designs and Decorations
Feather Flowers

By Carl Caronia

With a bit of ingenuity you can transform household feather dusters into sunflowers, tulips, hibiscus, wild roses or even flowers of your imagination.

The sunflower shown on the left below was made from the individual feathers of a yellow and orange duster. To make the centre of the sunflower you need: a circle 10 to 12 cm in diameter, cut from stiff cardboard; package of split peas, rice, or any small hard beans; white glue; spray tin of stain or clear varnish; pipe cleaner, and a desk stapler. Thirty feathers from the duster will each be attached to the stem with floral wire. Self-sticking green floral tape will be wound around a 45 cm garden stake to make the stem. Six leaves for the sunflower stem can be made from crepe paper or green feathers, or you can use artificial leaves from a discarded arrangement. Tendrils can be made by covering floral wire with brown tape and curling the ends around a pencil.

Fold a pipe cleaner in half and bend 2.5 cm of each tip outwards to form a T shape. Staple these tips to the back of the cardboard disc (Figure L). Glue beans on to cover the surface of the disc. When the glue is dry, spray the beans with varnish. Slant the disc at a 45-degree angle. Wrap the loop end of the pipe cleaner around the stake and spiral-wrap green floral tape around both.

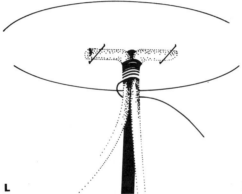

L

Figure L: Staple bent tips of a pipe cleaner to the bottom side of cardboard circle. Wrap floral wire around stake tip and pipe cleaner. Twist remaining pipe cleaner around the stake.

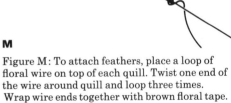

M

Figure M: To attach feathers, place a loop of floral wire on top of each quill. Twist one end of the wire around quill and loop three times. Wrap wire ends together with brown floral tape.

Cut the feathers loose at their bases from the duster handle with scissors, beginning with the outer row and gradually working inwards. Bend floral wire in half and place it on top of the base of a quill. Wind one end of the wire tautly around the quill three times (Figure M). Keep winding the remaining portion of this end of the wire around the other end of the wire. Cover each quill and its stem wire with green floral tape.

Space 10 orange feathers evenly around the centre disc so that the end of each one extends about 2.5 cm beyond the edge of the disc. Bind the wires of these feathers to the garden stake stem with green floral tape. Next mount floral wires on each quill of 20 yellow feathers of about the same size, and round the feather tips with manicure scissors. Arrange 10 yellow feathers around the disc, with about 5 cm of the yellow feathers showing beyond the first row of orange feathers. Tape the stems of this second row to the stick stem. Then tape a final row of 10 yellow feathers to the stem under the second row. Cover the entire stem with green tape, attaching artificial green leaves or tendrils at intervals, as in the photograph on the left. Feathers attached to wires can be shaped to fill in gaps along edge.

To complete, cover a tin with decorative paper. Fill with blocks of plastic foam to support the sunflower stem and cover the top with artificial moss.

Split peas and colourful feathers from a household duster were used for this sunflower which can be used as a gift, a party centrepiece or to decorate a kitchen windowsill.

Orange tulips, two-tone hibiscus and yarn-centred wild roses were made from feather dusters.

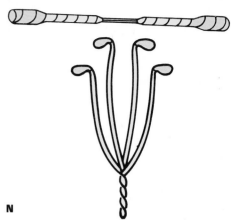

N

Figure N: To form the tulip or hibiscus stamens, bind two floral wires together with four turns of brown tape, thickly covering 2 cm at each end. Wrap remaining wires with one turn of green tape, leaving 2.5 cm in the middle bare, as top illustration shows. Wrap another pair of wires in the same way. Bend both pairs of wires in half at the centre and twist the uncovered joints together. Bend each brown tip at a right angle and the stamens are complete.

Tulips and hibiscus

For the orange tulips and two-tone hibiscus pictured above, you will need: red, yellow, and orange feather dusters; a roll of green floral tape; two dozen lengths of floral wire; one dozen stem wires; and artificial leaves.

To make the stamens at the centre of each flower, place two floral wires together and wrap 2 cm in from each end with four turns of brown tape (Figure N). Where the brown tapes stop, start wrapping with one turn of green tape towards the centre of the wires, but leave 2.5 cm uncovered in the middle. Repeat the process with another pair of floral wires. Then, fold both taped pairs in half, and twist the uncovered sections of wire together several times. Bend the brown tip of each stamen outwards at a 90-degree angle. Place the twisted joint of the stamens beside a stem wire and tape the two together with the green floral tape.

To complete the feather tulip, cut seven orange feathers and attach them to floral wires, as shown in Figure M, opposite. Cut each feather of the tulip to a point with scissors (see orange tulips in photograph above). Space the orange feathers evenly about the stamens, and secure them to the stem, using green tape. Wrap the entire stem with green floral tape. Then bind the wire bases of three slender artificial leaves spaced along the stem with green floral tape.

To make the hibiscus, proceed as you would for the tulip; however, instead of orange feathers, use the tips of five red feathers, 5 cm long, in the first row, and five yellow feathers, 10 cm long, spaced evenly underneath.

Wild rose

Three-ply, yellow ochre-coloured wool yarn is needed to make the centres of the roses in the photograph above. Wind the wool around four fingers 12 times. Gather the wool together by wrapping floral wire around the midpoint of the wool and twisting the wire on itself several times. With scissors, cut all the wool loops apart to form fringe (Figure O). Place twisted wire ends alongside a stem wire and tape the two together. Attach floral wires to five red feathers (see Figure M, opposite). Space each feather petal around the trimmed, fringed centre. Join feathers to the stem with green floral tape, then continue to wrap entire stem. Position leaves along stem and bind them in with green tape.

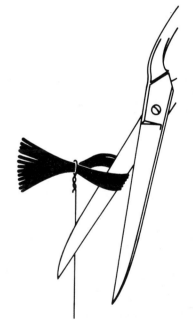

O

Figure O: To form a fringed centre for the wild rose, secure a dozen loops of yarn in the centre with floral wire; then cut through the loops.

Both roses are formed around cotton-ball centres covered with red crepe paper as described in the text. Large rose has six small, seven large petals; small rose has two small, two large petals.

Paper Folding and Cutting
Crepe Paper Flowers

The elasticity of crepe paper makes this material ideal for stretching and sculpting into more natural floral formations. The rose (left) and tulip (opposite) were made with red, yellow and green crepe paper, white glue with a brush, floral wire, stem wire or garden stakes, white and green floral tape, cotton balls and scissors. The patterns shown (Figures P, Q and R below, and T and U on page 22) are actual size, so simply trace them on to cardboard. Then cut out the cardboard, trace around it on the crepe paper and cut out the paper whose grain should run along the length of the petals and leaves.

Rose

To make the centre for a rose, cover a cotton ball with a piece of red crepe paper, close the opening with a floral wire and attach it to a stem wire with green floral tape. For the large rose shown in the photograph (left), cut six small petals and seven large petals from red crepe paper following the patterns in Figure P. For the small rose shown, cut two small and two large petals. Place your thumbs in the middle of each petal and cup it by stretching the crepe paper outwards (photograph 4), then bend the tips of each petal backwards by rolling the paper (photograph 5) much as you would curl a ribbon. The curved petals will stand away from the centre like those of a fresh rose. Use a brush to apply white glue 2.5 cm from the base area of each small petal. Hold the bud on the wire upside down and begin to glue on small petals first; then do the larger petals. Be sure to space the petals evenly around the centre. Avoid getting glue on the outside of the flower. When all petals have been attached, accordion-fold a 8 by 50 cm piece of green crepe paper, as in Figure B, page 15, for the calyx (cup-like leaves at the base of each flower).

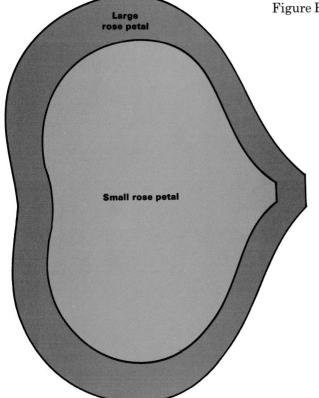

Large rose petal

Small rose petal

P

Figure P: Rose petals are made by tracing these shapes. For the small petal pattern follow the inside curved line, for the large petal pattern follow the outside curved line.

Q

Figure Q: Cut this curved shape from the accordion-folded crepe paper to make calyx to cup each flower. Cut only along dotted lines, leaving base area of folded paper joined.

R

Figure R: Cut four of these rose leaves for the stem of each rose. Then, glue a wire between each pair of leaves so you can attach them to the stem and position them easily.

4: Cup each rose petal by stretching the crepe paper with your thumbs in an outward motion.

5: Use a scissor blade or the side of a pencil to curl the edges of the rose petals outwards.

With supporting wire loops in each petal (see Figure S), and wire sandwiched into each leaf, you can mould this crepe paper tulip with ease.

Each pleat should be about 2.5 cm wide. To make the calyx, cut along the curved dotted lines shown in Figure Q (opposite) leaving about 2 cm of the folded paper still joined at the base of the calyx. Unfold the stack of crepe paper, and spread white glue 1 cm from the joined base of the paper. Wrap the calyx around the bottom of the large outer flower petals.

Next, cut two pairs of leaves from green crepe paper (Figure R). Glue each pair with a wire sandwiched vertically between. Allow 5 cm of wire to protrude.

In a spiral motion, wrap the entire stem with green floral tape. Start taping at the base of the calyx and work downwards. Attach the leaves to the stem at intervals by wrapping each wire joint in with tape. Freshen the completed rose petals and leaves by shaping them with the edge of a scissor blade or your fingertips. One or two romantic roses will look attractive in a crystal bud vase. A grouping of roses designed in contrasting colours can be secured in a foam block that has been placed in the bottom of a tall container.

Tulip

Actual-size pattern for tulip leaves and petals shown above, right, are given in Figures T and U on page 22. These patterns can also be used to make fabric flowers, using the methods described on page 22. Make stamens in the same way as for the feather tulip (Figure N, page 19). Bind the twisted wire of the stamen base to a garden stake with spiral-wrapped green floral tape. Cover four individual floral wires with white floral tape so the wire will not show through the yellow crepe paper petals. Bend each wire in half and form an oval loop (Figure S), and twist wire tips together to close.

Cut eight tulip petal patterns from yellow crepe paper (Figure U, page 22). Sandwich each wire loop (Figure S) between a pair of petals and glue in place. Space the four completed petals evenly about the stamens. Join the petal wires and stamen wires to the garden stake with floral tape. Glue one side of a 2 by 50 cm piece of green crepe paper and spiral wrap it around the entire stem. The wire inside each petal will allow you to bend it upwards. Curl petal tips with the side of a pencil.

Cut four slender leaf patterns (Figure T, page 22). Sandwich a wire 23 cm long between each of the two pairs, so that it runs down the centre of the leaves but stops about 4 cm from the leaf tip. Attach one leaf to the stem 12 cm down from the petals by wrapping and gluing a piece of green crepe paper around the wire joint. Place the second leaf 5 cm below the juncture of the first leaf and stem. Cover the second leaf joint and the remainder of the stem with crepe paper. Bend the leaves so that they branch and curl as in the colour photograph above, right. Fix your tulip into a block of plastic foam that has been placed within a clay pot. Cover the foam with moss.

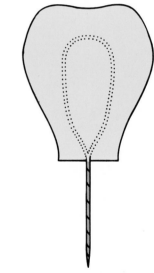

S

Figure S: A supporting wire loop is sandwiched between two tulip petals. Bend a floral wire wrapped with white tape to make the oval loop. Twist the ends of the wire together; then glue on the petals with the loop between.

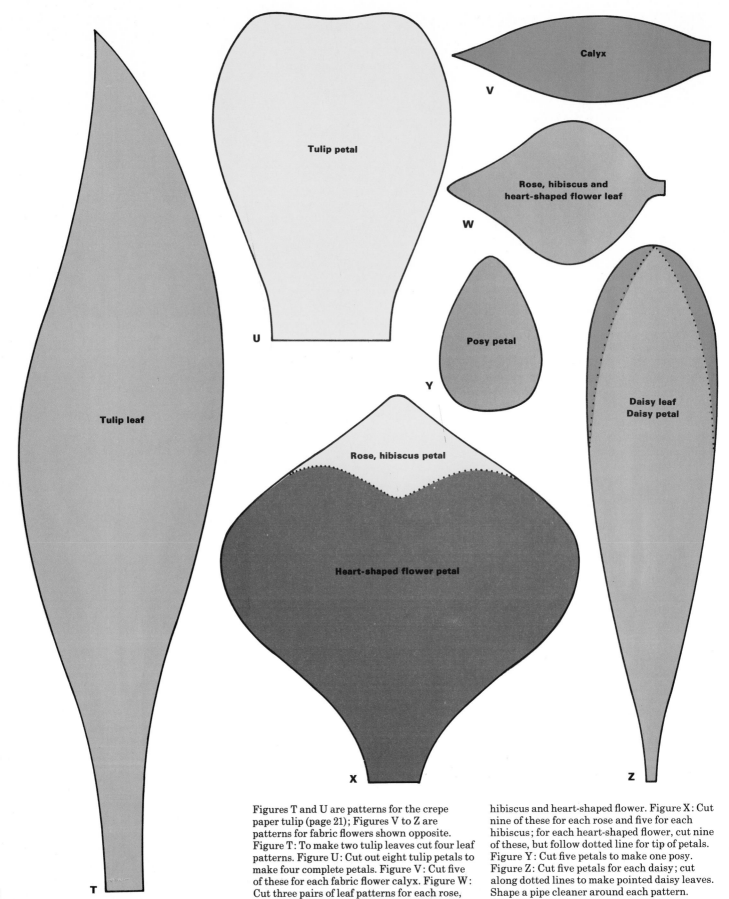

Calyx

V

Tulip petal

Rose, hibiscus and
heart-shaped flower leaf

W

Posy petal

Y

Daisy leaf
Daisy petal

Tulip leaf

U

Rose, hibiscus petal

Heart-shaped flower petal

X

Z

T

Figures T and U are patterns for the crepe paper tulip (page 21); Figures V to Z are patterns for fabric flowers shown opposite. Figure T: To make two tulip leaves cut four leaf patterns. Figure U: Cut out eight tulip petals to make four complete petals. Figure V: Cut five of these for each fabric flower calyx. Figure W: Cut three pairs of leaf patterns for each rose, hibiscus and heart-shaped flower. Figure X: Cut nine of these for each rose and five for each hibiscus; for each heart-shaped flower, cut nine of these, but follow dotted line for tip of petals. Figure Y: Cut five petals to make one posy. Figure Z: Cut five petals for each daisy; cut along dotted lines to make pointed daisy leaves. Shape a pipe cleaner around each pattern.

This basketful of gingham flowers shows the petal shapes you can use to make imaginative roses, daisies, hibiscus or simple posies.

Designs and Decorations
Fabric Flowers

Scraps of left-over fabrics are ideal for making cloth flowers. You can co-ordinate flower colours with curtains or bedspreads for a special effect. Or you can create a patchwork design by using a variety of fabrics in one flower.

To make eight of these flowers of gingham (as pictured above) or other fabric, you will need 45 cm of material; 4 cm wide cloth ribbon; five dozen chenille or extra-thick pipe cleaners; three dozen floral wires; one dozen stem wires; green floral tape; white glue with brush; 1.25 m of yellow ochre-coloured wool yarn; and scissors. Select a container which will harmonize with the arrangement. Place a foam block cut to size within the vase to support flower stems.

The centre of a rose is a plastic foam sphere about 2.5 cm in diameter, covered with 10 cm square fabric (photograph 6). The posy's centre is a small wad of cotton, covered with 5 cm square fabric. To secure the material, wrap a floral wire around the base twice. Make a daisy centre of yarn as you did the wild rose centre (Figure O, page 19). A hibiscus centre is made with three pipe cleaners. Using your thumb and forefinger, wind each end of each pipe cleaner on itself four times. Fold the pipe cleaner in half to create two stamens with curled ends. Fold the second pipe cleaner at one-quarter its length and the third at one-third its length to vary the length of the stamens. Attach completed stamens to a stem wire with green floral tape.

Transfer petal, calyx and leaf patterns on to cardboard (Figures V to Z, opposite). Each cardboard pattern acts as an edge or template against which you can fit and shape a pipe cleaner. Bend a pipe cleaner in half; align the bend with the apex of each petal or leaf and shape the pipe cleaner around each edge of the template (Figure AA). Twist the pipe cleaner closed twice at the base of the pattern and clip any remaining pipe cleaner strands. Lay the ironed cotton fabric on a flat surface. Brush glue on to one side of the pipe cleaner and place it directly upon the material. When the glue dries, cut the petal or leaf from the fabric, following the pipe cleaner outline. Attach a floral wire to each petal and leaf (see Figure M, page 18). For each flower cut five separate calyx patterns from cloth ribbon. Space petals evenly around either the plastic sphere centre or the stamens (depending on the flower), and wrap in place with floral tape. Then glue calyx pieces around the base of the petals. The wire within the pipe cleaner will allow you to shape each petal and leaf. Complete wrapping the stem and attaching leaves with floral tape.

6: To make the centre of a rose, hibiscus, or a flower with heart-shaped petals, push a stem wire through a 2.5 cm plastic foam sphere and cover it with a piece of fabric. Wrap a floral wire below the sphere to secure the cloth to the wire stem.

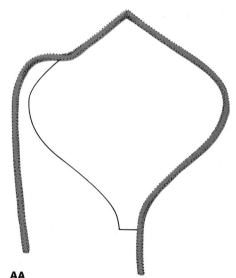

AA

Figure AA: To make pipe-cleaner frame that will hold fabric taut, bend cleaner in half; with bend at apex of flower or leaf, shape cleaner around perimeter of each petal and leaf pattern. Twist pipe cleaner closed at petal base. 23

FRAMING

Completing the Picture

By Beth Wigren

An early use of framing to complement paintings developed in Italy in the 13th century. The actual painting surface was hollowed out of a wood panel and the edges of the panel were left at the original level to form the frame. During the Renaissance, the idea of frames as added embellishments came into being. The early Renaissance frame was a small raised edge on each side of a flat panel, but many frames of the later Renaissance used more elaborate mouldings that were large, richly carved and gilded. A common finish in Renaissance times was gold leaf on gesso, a plaster mixture applied to seal the wood. In Colonial America, the settlers made bevelled mouldings from native woods, such as maple and pine. Today many frames have returned to the unadorned simplicity of the early Renaissance.

Harmony of picture and frame is governed by scale and proportion—the balance achieved by the picture and the frame. There are no hard and fast rules but there are several helpful guidelines. The width and depth of the moulding determines the visual weight of the frame; it should not seem so heavy that it overburdens the picture. The shape of the moulding is also important: a moulding with rounded edges works well with a picture having rounded shapes; an angular moulding blends with pictures having many straight lines or geometric shapes. The finish should also be compatible with the picture: a burnished wood frame matches warm colours, an antiqued frame goes well with an old print, a narrow black frame sets off a modern print, etching or photograph. Do not use too bright colours.

A mount, a border cut from heavy paperboard to separate the picture from the frame, creates a visual space that helps to isolate the picture; it is particularly useful for artwork that will hang on a wall that is patterned or brightly coloured. A mount also makes the finished size larger and more important, if that is the effect you want.

Sometimes artwork is mounted on a stiff board of paper or foam at least 6 mm thick; this kind of mounting will support needlework or keep a photograph smooth and flat. Glass is used as a protective covering for a work that might be damaged by dust. Non-reflective glass is available at a glazier; it is more expensive but worth the money if the picture is going to be in direct sunlight or strong indoor light. Glass is not usually used with a textured work such as an oil painting or heavy needlework where the glass could not lie flat against the surface of the artwork.

Furniture and Finishes
Basic Wood Moulding

The basic wood frame consists of four pieces of moulding joined at the corners with 45-degree mitred joints. This moulding has a rabbet—a notch along the inside edge of the back to receive the picture and glass (Figure A). You can buy picture-frame moulding in various lengths at frame shops and timber yards. You can also make frames from standard trim mouldings—the kind used around windows and doors or between wall and ceiling. These are available in a variety of shapes at any timber yard and cost less than frame mouldings. Some mouldings are shaped in such a way that angle can be used as the rabbet; others have to be combined so that a rabbet is formed. If you have a power saw, it is easy to cut a rabbet. Figure B shows cross sections of many of

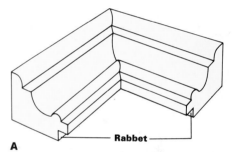

A   **Rabbet**

Figure A: Traditional picture frame moulding is constructed with a rabbet, the notch that holds the picture and glass.

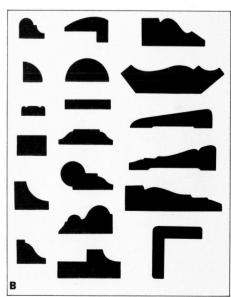

B

Figure B: Some of the standard millwork trim moulding shapes that can be used for framing; they are available from most timber suppliers.

Several examples of frames (left) include metal and wood frames that are pre-mitred, or cut to a 45-degree angle at the end. The metal frame has a polished silver-tone finish while the various woods have been painted, stained or simply left natural.

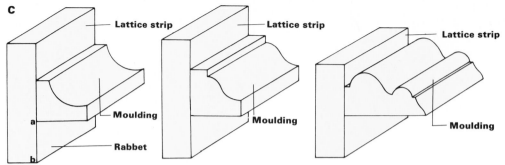

Figure C: Make frame moulding with standard millwork trim moulding by gluing a lattice strip to the moulding to form the rabbet. Measure the combined thickness of the picture, mounting board, glass and backing to determine the distance from a to b, the depth of the rabbet needed.

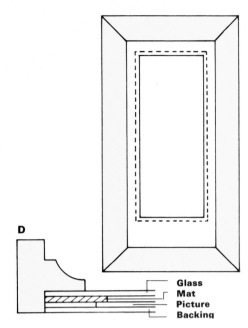

D

Figure D: Above, the mat overlaps the picture at least 6 mm on all sides. Below, the frame overlaps the mat at least 6 mm on all sides.

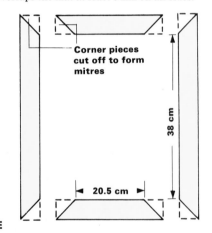

Figure E: If the overall length and width of the mount (after subtracting twice the rabbet width) is 38 by 20.5 cm, the minimum amount of 5 cm wide moulding needed is 30.5 cm for the top and the bottom and 48.5 cm for each side, or a total for all sides of 15.8 cm. When buying the moulding, allow a little extra for waste.

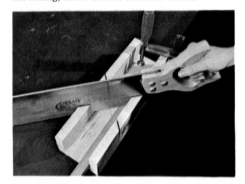

1: Clamp mitre box to work table and use tenon saw to cut 45-degree angles. Use scrap wood to support rabbet while cutting.

the common millwork mouldings. Figure C shows millwork mouldings (as shown in Figure B, page 25) in several combinations that create a rabbet.

The first step in making a frame is to decide if you want a mount around the picture (Figure D). To determine size, lay your picture on mounting board, available at an art supply shop, and try placing the moulding on the board at various distances from the edges of the picture until you have what you feel is a pleasing balance of picture, mount and frame. You can make the mount width equal on all sides of the picture, but it is traditional to use a width one-third larger below the picture. Measure the length and width of the mounting board established by your arrangement, and add to it the amount that the moulding will overlap the board on all sides. This will give you the mount measurements and also those for the cardboard backing and the glass.

The opening in the mount will be the size of the picture minus the mount overlap on the sides. If you are framing a white bordered photograph, for example, the mount opening should be 6 to 10 mm smaller on each side to cover the white border. Use a square and straight-edge to mark the opening in the mounting board. Then, using a knife or a single-edge razor blade with the straight-edge as a guide, cut out the opening in the mount. If you want a bevelled edge, use a heavy metal ruler with a bevelled edge and cut the board pressing the knife against the slant of the ruler.

Picture glass is thinner and clearer than window glass; you can buy glass cut to size from a glazier. If you cut the glass yourself, make sure the glass is perfectly clean and resting on a flat surface. Use a glass cutter (available in hardware shops) and a hard straight-edge. Hold straight-edge securely and, starting at the far end, draw glass cutter towards you with firm and constant pressure in one straight line. Never go over a cut a second time. To cut the glass after scoring, tap it gently on the reverse side at both ends of the cut (never in the middle) and separate the pieces by bending it slightly downwards.

To determine the amount of frame moulding needed, measure the length and width of the mounting board (or the picture if you are not using a mount) and subtract twice the width of the rabbet, the amount that the frame overlaps the picture (Figure E). Since the moulding is cut at 45-degree angles, you will need more moulding than simply the total of all four sides. Add the width of the moulding to the side measurement at each corner (Figure E) so the angle can be cut. This will give you the exact amount of moulding needed.

To make the frame in the photograph on page 27, I used moulding and a lattice strip. When gluing the moulding to the lattice strip, leave enough space under the moulding to form the rabbet (at least 6 to 10 mm). To find the exact rabbet depth, measure the combined thickness of the picture, mount, glass and backing. To cut the newly-formed moulding piece, measure side and top and bottom and cut the ends at 45-degree angles (Figure E). Use a mitre box and a tenon saw to make these cuts (photograph 1). Cut *all* angles before starting to join. When these moulding pieces are joined at the corner, the inside edges should form a right angle. If they do not, minor adjustments can be made by sanding the mitres slightly. When they fit properly, hold both

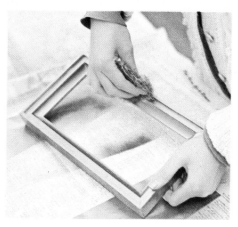

2: The finished frame was first painted with red enamel paint. When this red undercoat has dried, the frame is sprayed with gold paint.

3: Then the gold paint, when dry, is rubbed lightly with fine steel wool to let some of the red undercoat show through.

pieces in a vice and attach them with resin glue and small brads, two from one side and one from the other. Continue with each corner until all four are joined. Any gaps left in the mitres can now be filled with wood putty. Sand the frame and it is ready for paint or other finish. The procedure for applying the red-gold finish that I used is shown in photographs 2 and 3, above.

To assemble, position the picture in the mount opening and secure it all around with masking tape. Put the glass, the mount with the picture, and the cardboard backing in the frame. To hold everything in place, turn the frame on edge and drive tiny brads into the frame's rabbet on the side that is down. Turn the frame and drive brads every 10 cm along each side. Apply masking tape to seal the space between cardboard backing and frame; this will keep out dust. Measure one-third of the distance from the top of the frame down each side, insert tiny screw eyes and attach a light wire between them. When pulled taut, the wire should reach to about 3 cm below the top of the frame.

This frame is made with moulding glued to a lattice strip. The steps in painting the frame are shown in photographs 2 and 3 (left). The warm gold colour with a red undercoat harmonizes with the colours in the picture.

Furniture and Finishes
Metal Frame

The modern look of a metal frame is appropriate for photographs, abstract paintings or modern needlework in contemporary room settings. A metal frame is basically the same as a wood frame except that the mitred corners are joined by metal clips rather than being nailed or glued; and the glass, picture and backing are held in place with spring clips instead of brads.

Pre-mitred metal mouldings are made of aluminium and come in several finishes. The mouldings also come in wood and plastic finishes, but these may not be as readily available. The mouldings are sold in packages containing two pieces of moulding of the same length, corner clips and back spring clips. Two packages, one for the sides and one for the top and bottom, are needed to make one frame. The size shown on the package is the inside measurement, the length of the edge which will be next to the mount or picture. Follow the assembly directions on the package.

Metal frame mouldings can be sawn to odd sizes. If, for example, you want the inside edge of the moulding to be 34.3 cm long, buy the next larger size and cut it down, using a mitre box and a metal-cutting hack saw. You can spray paint the frame in any colour you choose.

Glass, mount and backing cardboard should be cut to fit inside the frame. They are held in place by spring clips which bridge the corners. Some use screws; others clip into the moulding. Metal moulding systems include special clips to hold the hanging wire. Use the screws provided to screw these into the groove in the back of the frame and string a wire between them.

The impact of the primary colours of red and blue and the clearly defined shapes of this modern print are enhanced by the straight, thin lines of the metal frame.

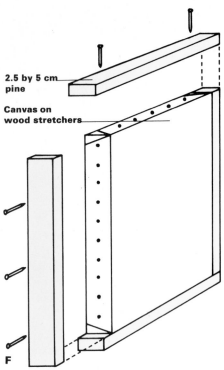

2.5 by 5 cm pine

Canvas on wood stretchers

F

Figure F: A simple stick frame can be made with wood strips nailed directly to the wooden "stretchers" used to hold the canvas taut.

Furniture and Finishes
Stick Frames

Easily assembled stick frames can be made with simple, unadorned wood strips available at any timber yard. They are informal, so they go well with casual room settings. Joints are butted instead of mitred, thus calling for much less precision in woodworking. At its simplest, a stick frame is merely a wood border nailed directly to canvas stretchers, the wood supports of an oil painting (Figure F). Or a stick frame can be a combination of lattice and pine as shown in Figure G, and the photograph below. I framed a paper print by first gluing it to a block of 2 cm thick plywood. Plywood, tempered hardboard, and pressed wood are good because they resist warping. A colour illustration from a magazine can be attached to a piece of plywood several ways. One is the white-glue-and-varnish method. Start by cutting the plywood to size with a fine-tooth saw that will not leave a ragged edge. Trim the magazine illustration to the same dimensions as the plywood. Dilute white glue, using two parts glue to one part water and brush on to the back of the illustration. Turn it over carefully and lay it on the plywood, using the palm of your hand to smooth out air bubbles. Leave face up for 20 minutes until the glue dries. You can make the illustration more durable by coating it with varnish. Build up several coats, allowing each to dry before applying the next.

Alternatively, there are several commercial products that you can use. One makes a plastic transfer out of printed material by the application of several coats of the liquid. When dry, the paper can be peeled off the plastic and the ink will remain embedded in the plastic. The transfer can then be glued to the wood. This cannot be used on glossy photographs, engraved invitations or varnished paper. Another product, a combination adhesive/sealer for decoupage work, combines the gluing and varnishing steps in one procedure.

Another version of a stick frame, made with lattice strips and 2.5 by 5 cm pine boards, is an inexpensive frame for an illustration from a magazine mounted on 2 cm plywood. The method of construction is shown in Figure G.

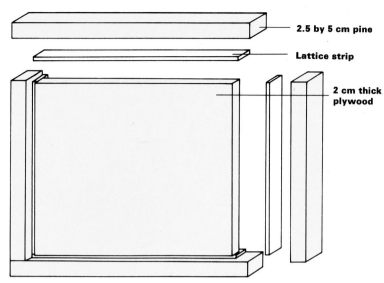

G

Figure G: Mount the lattice strips so the front of the plywood extends 6 mm beyond the lattice strips. Mount outside 2.5 by 5 cm pine pieces so they extend 6 mm in front of the picture.

Once the picture is in place and protected with finish, paint plywood edges a colour that will contrast with the colour of the frame. In this case white gesso was used. Next, cut 6 mm by 2.8 cm lattice strips to lengths to fit around the plywood rectangle; the vertical pieces match the height of the plywood and the horizontal pieces extend to cover ends of the vertical pieces (Figure G). Nail these pieces to the plywood edges so they are recessed 6 mm in from the front of the plywood backing on which the picture is mounted. Paint front edges of the lattice strips with white gesso. Then cut the 2.5 by 5 cm outer frame pine pieces to fit around the recessed frame. Paint inside surfaces of the pine pieces with white gesso. Then nail pine pieces around the lattice frame, with top and bottom pieces overlapping side pieces as shown. Let the front edges protrude 6 mm in front of the picture surface (Figure G). Paint the front edges and outside faces of the outer pine pieces a colour that harmonizes with the picture. Put screw eyes into the plywood back one-third of the way down from the top to hold the hanging wire, and the frame is finished.

Furniture and Finishes
Weathered Wood Frame

Using weathered wood as a background frame for a photograph as shown above right, provides an interesting blend of colours and materials.

Photographic colour prints should be mounted on 6 mm foam core board. With a single-edge razor blade, cut the mounting board and the photograph at the same time so the edges match, and paint the edges of both the print and the mount black. Mount the photograph with special spray adhesive for photographs which is available at art supply or camera shops. Spray the back of the photograph and the mount, wait until almost dry and press the photograph in place. Weight the photograph down for 3 minutes until the adhesive is dry. Cut a piece of 6 mm foam board 2.5 cm less in each dimension than the photograph, to use as a spacer between the mounted photograph and the weathered board. Position the photograph so the background board provides an attractively balanced mount effect all around the print and mark the position lightly in pencil. Then centre the spacer in this marked area and attach it to the wood with glue or small nails (Figure H). Attach the photograph's foam core board to the spacer with white glue and join them to line up with the pencil marks. Leave the assembly face up for several minutes until the glue dries. Then add a screw eye to the centre of the wood top.

A three-dimensional effect is created by placing a 6 mm thick spacer between the photograph of a girl in a garden (which has been mounted on foam core board) and weathered wood.

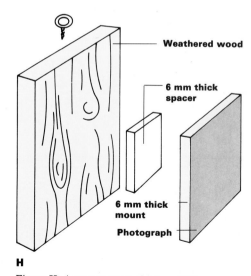

H

Figure H: A spacer, 6 mm thick and 2.5 cm smaller in length and width than the foam core board backing for a photograph, is positioned between the photograph and weathered wood.

29

A refinished antique typecase is filled with dried beans, pasta, dried flowers, old bottles and buttons, and bits of ribbon and fabric to create a nostalgic box frame.

Furniture and Finishes
A Box Frame

Small three-dimensional objects can be displayed and preserved within a box frame. Such frames are often used to display collections of coins or butterflies. Box frames may be built in two ways. One way uses a moulding with a deep rabbet, a spacer between the glass and the background, and some method of holding the samples against the background (Figure I). The other has glass held in place by corner pieces (photograph opposite). As the drawings below show, you can use stock mouldings to frame the display and hold the glass.

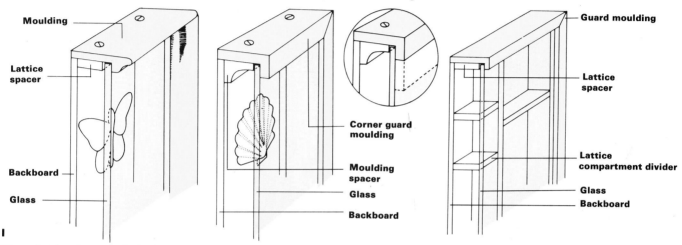

Figure I: A box frame can be built with the glass held between a moulding and spacer strip, as on the left. Or you can use a moulding and corner guard moulding to hold glass (centre) and trim off one side of corner guard as shown in the inset. A compartmented box frame (right) has an assembly of lattice-strip shelves added to the basic unit.

To make a box frame, cut the mouldings first, mitre the corners, and fasten them together with glue and brads. Cut a backboard of plywood so that it will fit inside the frame, then set it aside. Have picture glass cut to fit inside frame against the inside rabbet created by the frame moulding. Then cut spacer strips to fit inside the box frame against the glass. These can be lattice strips or moulding. With frame face down, put the glass in place and press the spacers against it to hold it tight. Clamp the spacers in place while you fasten them to the moulding frame with two or three screws on each side, turned in from the outside. Drill pilot holes for flat-headed screws and counter-sink the heads so they are flush; they must be short enough not to show inside the box. The backboard may be left exposed or covered with a background material suitable for the objects being displayed. Objects being displayed can be attached to the backboard with pins if you use a glued-on fabric. Or you can use wires through the backboard, or screws driven into the backboard, or simply glue the objects to the board. Use any method that will hold them securely while the box is in a vertical position. To secure the backboard to the frame, place brads flat against the backboard and tap them into the moulding.

Box frames need not have only one compartment. For example, an old typecase can be refinished and used to display small objects on a wall, as in the photograph opposite. Here, the compartments are varied in size for a pleasing effect. The pasta and dried beans contrast nicely with the old bottle and buttons. The glass fits on top of compartment dividers and inside the outer frame, where it is held in place by brass corners.

You can build your own compartmented box frame. Use the construction described above, but add lattice strips, nailed and glued together, to make compartment dividers. The shelving should be built as a single assembly that will slip inside the box frame from the rear and rest securely against the glass. Simple butted joints, glued and fastened with wire brads, will do the job.

FUR RE-CYCLING
New Uses for Old Fur

By Lee K. Thorpe

Old fur garments, too worn to wear but too good to discard, hang idly in many a cupboard and are forgotten in many an attic trunk. They can also be bought inexpensively at second-hand clothing shops. There are many new things you can make from a shabby old fur coat. You might shorten it into a jacket and make cushions from the left-over fur. Or you can turn it into one or more fur accessories: matching collar and cuffs; a fluffy, two-metre-long stole; a muff, hat or an unusual bag.

You do not need to be an expert seamstress to salvage an old coat for a new use. A novice can make a fine fur cushion. Once you learn the basic differences between working with fur and working with fabric, you will be able to get new life out of fur garments that other people might discard as useless.

Fur's unique qualities make it an excellent material to re-cycle. Unlike fabric, fur can be pieced together so that no seams show—since they are hidden by hair. This means you can cut and piece all the good sections from a worn coat and have material that looks like one piece. One important difference between fur and fabric is that fur is sewn without a seam allowance. Seams are butted rather than overlapped, so you cut pattern pieces to their finished size. (Fake fur consists of a face or pile with a knitted or woven back. It requires a seam allowance like any other fabric.) Note, too, that you mark fur on the skin side and cut it with the skin side up. Marking done with a felt-tipped pen will not show through.

Tools and materials

For all the projects on the following pages you will need: a craft knife or single-edge razor blade; a leather needle with a three-sided wedge-shaped point (called a glover's needle), available at haberdashery counters or craft supply shops; thimble; pins; heavy-duty cotton or nylon thread; masking tape; felt-tipped pen. In addition, you will need an adhesive seam binding such as insulating tape or sticking plaster. You can substitute stay tape or seam binding, but it will require an extra sewing step (see Craftnotes, page 35). For some projects you will also need cotton domette, grosgrain ribbon, and material for lining. Velvet is recommended for backing the stole on page 41.

Basic techniques

Testing: Some areas of an old coat may be too worn or too weak to withstand a reconstruction job. To test the strength of an old fur, yank the hair of the fur in several places. If hairs do not pull out easily, the fur is probably usable. Also check the dryness of the skin. To do this, open the lining of the coat along the hemline and pinch the skin side in several places. If it seems powdery or brittle, it is probably too dry to re-cycle into a new garment, although it might be used as a cushion cover. Another test of suppleness is to moisten a small area of skin and stretch it. If it stretches without tearing, the skin is in good condition. Fur that is still good but has a weak backing can be used with lightweight fabric sewn in for support.

Stitching: Beginners will find it best to stitch fur seams by hand, so the following projects call for careful hand sewing. A sharp glover's needle is recommended because it will pierce the skin more readily than ordinary needles. It is true that furriers use a sewing machine and feed the fur into it edge to edge; your sewing machine might achieve the same effect with a tiny zigzag stitch, using a special needle for sewing leather.

Cushions are a good beginning project involving the use of fur remnants. The designs can be adapted to the size, shape and colour of available materials. They are easy to sew and are welcome gifts. Instructions for making the cushion with contrasting triangles begin on page 34.

Decorate with Fur

Fur-covered cushions like those pictured on the previous page can be made from a single piece of fur, from small scraps sewn together, or from furs of contrasting colours and textures. The fur front is joined to a vinyl, velvet, or suede cloth back, then this pocket is stuffed with a cushion form or loose filling. If you have never worked with fur, you will soon find that it is as easy to use as any other material, once you learn the basic techniques. Making a cushion introduces you to the method of cutting fur and to basic hand stitches.

Begin by experimenting with small pieces of fur, as for the chequered or triangle cushion. The size and type of cushion you decide to make depends on the kind and amount of fur you have. The finished triangle cushion (directions below) measures 30.5 cm on each side. To make it larger or smaller, adapt the directions accordingly. Fur can be pieced invisibly, so you can sew small pieces of identical fur together and they will look like one piece so long as the hair all points in one direction. Even if you make a patchwork cushion with different colours and types of fur, your finished piece will be smooth-looking if you stitch carefully when seaming.

Materials: In addition to the basic tools and materials listed on page 32, you will need: a 30.5 cm square of lightweight cotton cloth if you need to support an unevenly worn or fragile skin; four triangles of fur for the cushion front, each with a 30.5 cm base and 22 cm sides; a 30.5 cm square of vinyl, velvet, or suede cloth for the back; and a 30.5 cm square cushion form or stuffing.

Making the triangle cushion

First cut a triangular pattern from heavy cardboard. Make the base 30.5 cm and each side 22 cm. Place the pattern on the skin side and anchor it with a weight to keep it from slipping. Then trace the pattern on the skin with a felt-tipped pen. Cut out four fur triangles as shown in Figure A. When cutting, be sure to cut only the skin, not the hair.

For reinforcement, apply adhesive tape flush with the cut edges as in Figure B.

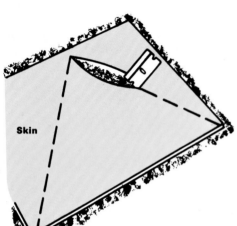

A

Figure A: Cut fur on the skin side, beginning at one corner of the triangle. Pierce the skin, then cut slowly towards yourself. Hold the blade at a 45-degree angle from the skin. With your other hand, raise skin as the cutting frees it.

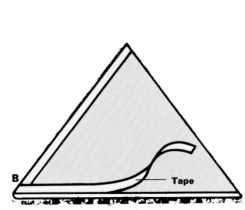

B

Figure B: To prevent stretching or tearing, tape the cut edges. Apply the adhesive tape flush with the edges on the skin side.

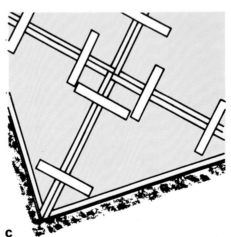

C

Figure C: Use strips of masking tape (shown in white) to hold fur triangles temporarily in place while you position them properly.

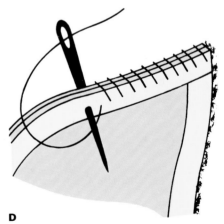

D

Figure D: With fur sides together, join two triangles by using the simple overhand-stitch shown. Join all four triangles the same way.

Stay tape or seam binding can be substituted (see Craftnotes, opposite). Position the four triangles together and use strips of masking tape to hold the pieces temporarily in place. Starting with two facing pieces, overhand-stitch all four triangles together (see Figure D). Use masking tape for tacking. As you sew, catch the adhesive tape in the seam and push stray hairs back to the fur side. Be sure that the four points match at the centre. Remove masking tape as you come to it.

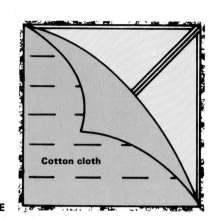

Figure E: Attach the cotton cloth to a weak skin with long running stitches in parallel rows 5 cm or so apart.

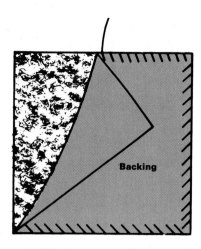

Figure F. With the cover inside out, overhand-stitch vinyl backing to the fur cushion front. Sew around three sides.

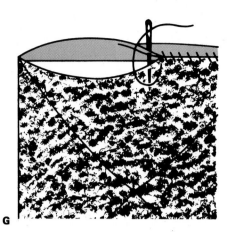

Figure G: Turn the cushion fur side out and insert cushion foam or stuffing. Overhand-stitch the seam closed with tiny stitches.

If you need lightweight cotton cloth to support worn or fragile skin, attach it to the skin side (Figure E) after joining the four fur triangles. Next, join the backing to the front by sewing around three sides (Figure F). Turn the cushion fur side out and stuff it. To finish, overhand-stitch the remaining seam on the fur side. These stitches will be hidden by the fur.

CRAFTNOTES: SEWING FUR

Tape is applied to the fur's cut edges to keep them from stretching and to reinforce seams. Use an adhesive tape, or sticking plaster. You can also use stay tape or seam binding. Either of these must be sewn in place, but will make the seams more durable; the extra stitching will not weaken the skin.

Apply adhesive tape flush with the skin's cut edge to reinforce it and prevent stretching.

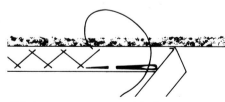

Stitch stay tape or seam binding to a cut fur edge with herringbone stitches (shown above) or even running stitches (right).

A glover's needle's wedge-shaped point (enlarged here), cuts cleanly through skin.

These hand stitches are the basic ones for sewing fur. Most sewing is done on the skin side. Pick up just enough of the skin to make a firm stitch.

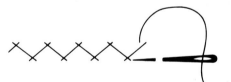

Herringbone stitch: Use this basic tacking stitch for attaching tape or interfacing, and for binding a fur edge with grosgrain ribbon.

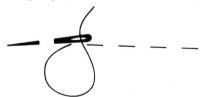

Even Running Stitch: Use for sewing on tape and for firm tacking. It is interchangeable with herringbone stitch.

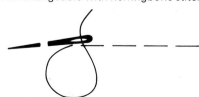

Uneven Running Stitch: Use for tacking interfacing. It is also interchangeable with herringbone stitch.

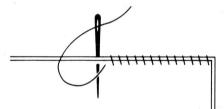

Overhand-stitch: Use to sew two pieces of fur together or to attach fabric to fur. It is interchangeable with blanket stitch.

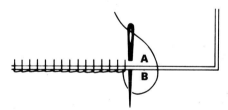

Blanket Stitch: For a stronger seam, use this instead of the overhand-stitch. Insert needle at A and bring out at B, with the needle in front of thread loop.

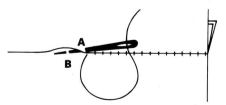

Slipstitch: To make the basic finishing stitch, insert needle at A and come out at B, just catching the under fabric.

Salvage an old coat by cutting it down to make a finger-tip length jacket; this is pieced mink.

Needlecrafts
Shortening a Coat

A new hemline can make a big difference in a garment. Examine any worn coat to see if you can cut it down to jacket length, short or long. Shortening introduces you to the turned-up hem, used at the bottom of fur jackets and coats. A strip of interfacing, cut from canvas or unbleached cotton, for example, is sewn in to give such a hem body, then the fur is turned up and secured in place. Grosgrain ribbon (a firm ribbed fabric) is sewn to the skin edge and serves both to bind the edge and to provide a means of anchoring the finished hem firmly in place.

Materials
In addition to the basic tools for fur work (page 32), you will need 1.5 cm-wide grosgrain ribbon and a strip of interfacing the length of the hem. This interfacing should be 5 cm wider than the hem; thus, a 7.5 cm-wide strip is right size interfacing for a 2.5 cm hem.

First, determine the length you want your jacket or coat to be. Using masking tape or safety pins on the skin side, make a temporary hem so you can get an idea of how the garment will look before you cut. Bear in mind that the finished garment will seem slightly longer than the turned-up length because hair will extend beyond the actual hem.

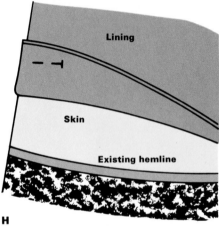

H

Figure H: Pull out the threads holding the coat's lining and pin it up out of the way. Some coats have a second loose lining which should also be pinned back.

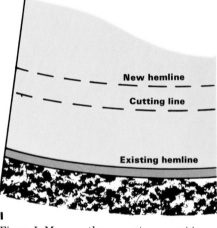

I

Figure I: Measure the amount you want to shorten from the existing hemline and mark the new length with a felt-tipped pen. Draw a line 2.5 cm below new hemline as cutting line.

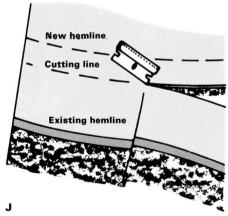

J

Figure J: Pierce the skin and cut towards you along the cutting line, slowly and carefully. Save the fur you remove for another use.

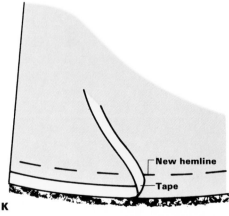

K

Figure K: Tape the new fur edge on the skin side. This will be overhand-stitched into the seam when grosgrain ribbon is applied.

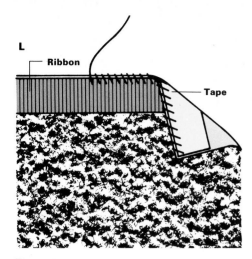

Figure L: Attach grosgrain ribbon on the fur side with an even overhand-stitch. Sew through all three thicknesses: ribbon, skin, and tape.

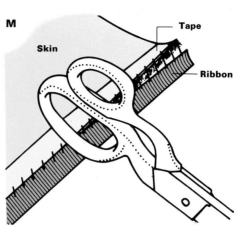

Figure M: Flatten the ribbon seam open by rubbing it with a scissors handle. This is also a good way to flatten seams joining two fur pieces.

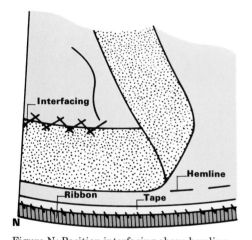

Figure N: Position interfacing above hemline and sew upper edge to the skin with herringbone stitches; lower edge need not be sewn.

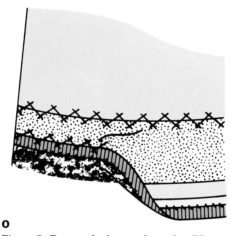

Figure O: Turn up fur hem and sew the ribbon to the body of the coat through the interfacing. Use a firm herringbone stitch.

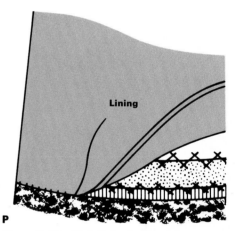

Figure P: Slipstitch lining in place after trimming it and allowing for a 6 mm hem. The lining should end 2.5 cm above the hemline.

Work on a flat surface and use a weight such as an iron or a book to keep the fur from slipping. Pin the lining out of your way (Figure H). Then mark the new hemline and a cutting line on the skin side with a felt-tipped pen (Figure I). A 2.5 cm wide hem is fine for most furs, but not all. You might want a wider hem if you plan to re-cycle your fur again at a later date. Consider the weight of the fur and make sure that the hem allowance, if wider than 2.5 cm, will not add too much bulk to the hem. The effect you want is a round, smooth look.

Cut off the excess fur (Figure J) and if it is not too worn, save it for another use. Reinforce the new fur edge with tape, applying it flush to the skin side (Figure K). To finish the edge, attach 1.5 cm-wide grosgrain ribbon, using overhand-stitch and working on the fur side (Figure L). Then flatten the ribbon seam open with a scissors handle (Figure M).

Attach a strip of interfacing to the skin (Figure N). The interfacing gives body to the hem and helps create a smooth, unbroken line. The interfacing should be the length of the hem and 5 cm wider than the hem allowance. Position it on the new hemline and sew the upper edge to the skin with running or herringbone stitches.

To hem, turn up the fur to the new hemline and sew the ribbon to the body of the coat using herringbone stitches (Figure O) or running stitches. The hem should be as smooth as possible.

The final step is to adjust the lining and sew it in place (Figure P). Measure and trim the lining so that it falls 2.5 cm above the hemline when you have turned it under 6 mm. Sew the lining to the lower ribbon edge with slipstitches.

A shawl collar can be worn on a jacket, coat or sweater. Here, a wide fox collar adorns a pierced fox jacket. Patterns for a narrower collar and cuffs are on the right below.

Needlecrafts
Fur Collar and Cuffs

A fur collar or a collar and cuffs set can be attached to a jacket, coat or long sweater. Making a collar and cuffs involves one of the trickier problems in fur re-cycling: laying a pattern so the hair falls properly. When your collar and cuffs are completed, the direction of the hair flow should be uniform for both collar pieces and for both cuffs. If you can, lay out the patterns for the two collar pieces so that the hair flows out and away from the neckline where the two pieces are joined at the centre back seam, as the arrow on the pattern indicates. The hair flow for the cuffs should be horizontal—around the cuff.

Try various ways of arranging pattern pieces on the fur so that the direction of the hair for the two collar pieces will be the same and the two cuffs will also be uniform. In most fur coats, the hair runs down. In flat furs, such as broadtail and Persian lamb, the hair twists in all directions. In sheared furs, such as sheared raccoon, nutria, rabbit, mole, beaver and lucea lamb, the texture is uniform and velvety, but you can discover the direction of hair flow by rubbing your hand on the fur to see which way the hair runs flatter. The flatter way is with the hair flow. Furs such as mink, musquash, and fox have an unmistakable hair flow.

Materials: You will need to make a trial pattern. Use heavy muslin or any cotton fabric. In addition to basic materials (page 32), you will need 2 cm wide grosgrain ribbon to bind all outside edges; cotton domette for padding; and satin or silk for the lining.

Making the patterns
Make cardboard or paper patterns for the collar and cuffs by enlarging those shown in Figure Q. Mark arrows on the patterns to indicate the direction of the hair flow. You will have to cut two collar pieces, reversing the pattern for the second piece so the collar curves properly. You may need to adjust the shape and size of the pattern pieces to suit your figure, your coat or sweater, and the fur you have available. Cuff widths generally range from 7.5 to 12.5 cm.

Figure Q: Enlarge the basic shawl collar and cuff patterns right (see page 49 for instructions on enlarging a pattern), then adjust them to suit the garment you have selected. Patterns have no seam allowance because fur pieces are joined edge to edge. Arrows suggest the direction of the fur's hair flow. Make a pattern for the left half of the collar, as illustrated, then turn it over and make a pattern for the right half. Cut one pattern piece for each cuff.

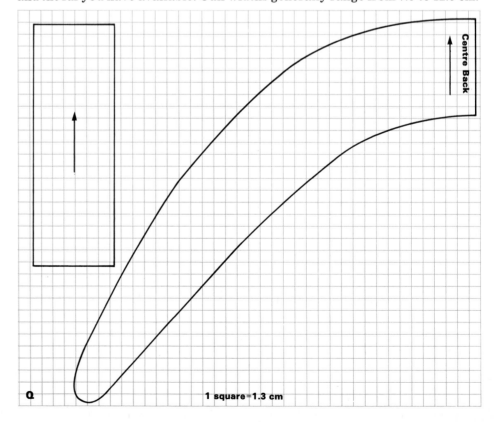

Q   1 square=1.3 cm

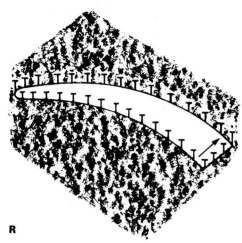

R

Figure R: To assure proper hair flow, first position paper pattern on fur side. To determine cutting line, pins are pushed through to skin side all around at 5 cm intervals.

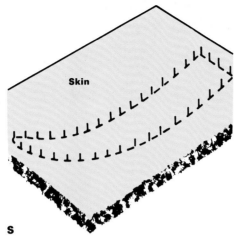

S

Figure S: Turn fur to the skin side and mark pin points with a felt-tipped pen. Then connect the points to indicate the cutting line. Cut each collar and cuff piece separately.

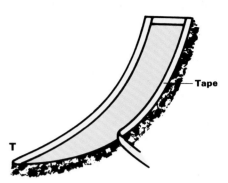

T

Figure T: Tape all cut edges to prevent stretching (see Craftnotes, page 35), after you have cut two collar pieces and one piece for each of the cuffs.

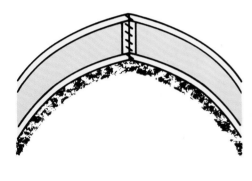

U

Figure U: Join collar pieces by holding fur sides together and overhand-stitching seam. Remember to catch tape with the thread as well. Flatten seam open as in Figure M, page 37.

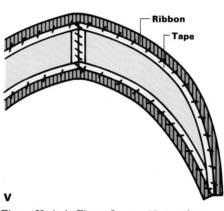

V

Figure V: As in Figure L, page 37, attach grosgrain ribbon to all outside edges and flatten open. This ribbon extension will later be folded over the skin and sewn in place for the hem.

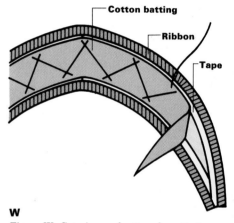

W

Figure W: Cut pieces of cotton domette 6 mm smaller all around than the fur pieces. Attach the domette pieces firmly to the skin with wide herringbone stitches.

Enlarging the cuff pattern in Figure Q will give you a 9 cm wide cuff. Using the enlarged paper patterns, cut trial pieces of heavy muslin or similar fabric. Try on the fabric collar and cuffs to see how they look. If any adjustments are necessary, revise the paper patterns before you start to work on the fur.

Assembling the collar and cuffs

Lay the fur you are re-cycling flat and position patterns pieces on the fur side to make sure the hair flows attractively. If you are working with an old coat, pin the lining out of your way. It is not necessary to take the whole coat apart—just free a large enough area of fur. Mark the fur by pushing straight pins through to the skin side at 5 cm intervals along the pattern edges (Figure R). Then turn the fur to the skin side and connect the pin marks with a felt-tipped pen to determine the cutting line. Cut out the fur pieces and tape all the raw edges (see Craftnotes, page 35), including the centre back seam edges. Next, using overhand-stitch, join the two collar pieces at the centre back, catching the tape with the thread. The hair flow should be the same on either side of the seam. With some furs hairs will overlap.

Working on the fur side, attach grosgrain ribbon to all edges, except for the centre neck seam where it is unnecessary (Figure V).

Prepare padding by cutting cotton domette 6 mm smaller all round than the fur collar and cuffs. Then tack it to the skin with herringbone stitches.

FUR CARE CRAFTNOTES

If your old coat is in poor condition, it could be due to improper care, as well as to age. Fur will stay in good condition for many years if it is cared for properly. These tips will help you to maintain fur pieces:
Do not leave fur near heat; the fur will dry out and the skin will become brittle and liable to split.
Hang fur garments on broad-shouldered hangers or padded hangers. Be sure to allow space around the garment for air to circulate.
Never store fur in a plastic bag.
Do not use chemical sprays to moth-proof fur.
If fur gets wet, shake it and hang it to dry in a cool place.

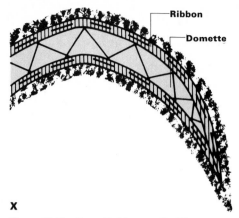
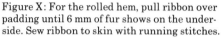
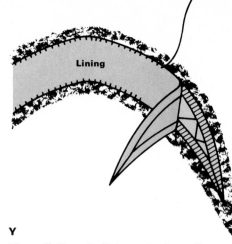

X

Figure X: For the rolled hem, pull ribbon over padding until 6 mm of fur shows on the underside. Sew ribbon to skin with running stitches.

Y

Figure Y: Turn the lining under 6 mm all around and sew it in place by slipstitching it to the grosgrain ribbon with tiny stitches.

Rolled hems will add a professional look to the outer edges of the collar and cuffs. To make a rolled hem, pull the grosgrain ribbon so that some of the fur (about 6 mm) rolls to the underside, and sew the ribbon to the skin at that point (Figure X). Overlap the ribbon at the collar points and the cuff corners so the hem lies smooth.

Cut the satin lining the same size as the fur pieces. Turn under a 6 mm hem all around and then slipstitch the lining in place (Figure Y).

To finish the cuffs, join the cuff ends with overhand-stitch. Match the cuff seam to the sleeve's inner seam if there is one. Pin, then slipstitch the cuffs to the sleeves along both edges to anchor them firmly in place; or since the cuffs are lined, you can also attach the upper cuff edge to the lower sleeve edge and have the cuff serve as an extension of the sleeve.

To attach the collar to a coat or sweater, pin it along the neckline as pictured below. Match the centre seam of the collar to the back centre seam of the garment if there is one. Pin the inner edge of the collar lining to the inner coat or sweater neckline. Slipstitch along the line of pins. Anchor firmly with extra stitches at the centre seam and around lower ends.

To make your collar and cuffs instantly removable when the garment needs cleaning, you can sew snap tape to the inside edge of the garment and to the collar and cuffs. However, a slipstitched set can be removed and sewn on another garment with little difficulty.

Collar and cuffs of racoon fur are pinned to the sweater, then slipstitched in place. Since they are fully lined, they can be sewn on the inside edges only. The set is then easy to detach.

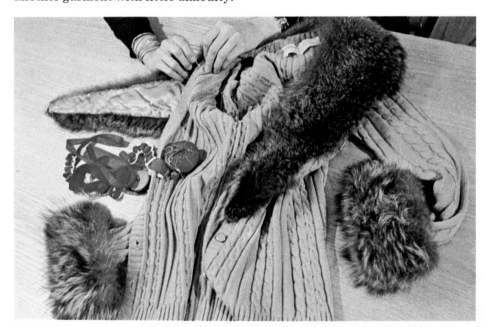

This two-metre-long fox stole has a velvet lining and rolled hems, giving it a soft, rounded look.

Needlecrafts
Have a Stole

A stole is made with the same techniques used for the collar and cuffs (pages 38 to 40). A worn jacket is likely to have enough usable fur to make a two metre-long stole but, whatever the source, you will have to do some piecing.

A stole can be any length, but most are from $1\frac{1}{2}$ to 2 metres. A good width is from 12.5 to 8 cm. The important thing is to make sure the hair flow is uniform for the entire length of the stole. Most stoles have a vertical flow.

When cutting an old fur coat or jacket into sections of a stole, try to cut long pieces. Then you will have fewer sections to piece together. Make sure you have the same number of pieces on each side of the centre back, so that when you wear the stole it will fall evenly, front and back. For example, if you make a two metre long stole, cut four pieces to make a 50 cm long strip, and four pieces for another strip the same length. When the two strips are joined, they will look uniform.

Materials: In addition to basic tools on page 32, you will need cotton domette for padding; 1.5 cm wide grosgrain ribbon for edges; velvet for backing.

First, study and measure the jacket or coat you are re-cycling to make sure you have enough usable fur. Then cut and arrange pieces in a line, with uniform hair flow, until you have a piece the desired length. Tape all the edges (see Craftnotes, page 35), and sew the seams as shown in Figure D, page 34. Flatten seams with scissors handle, as shown in Figure M, page 37.

Cut cotton domette 2.5 cm smaller than the fur all around. Position the domette on the skin side and tack with wide herringbone stitches, as in Figure W, page 39. Next, sew grosgrain ribbon to all the outside fur edges as outlined for the collar and cuffs project. Flatten seams.

Make rolled hems following the directions given for the collar and cuffs. At least 6 mm of fur should show on the underside.

Cut a velvet backing 6 mm larger than the fur all around. It will be necessary to piece the velvet. You can do this on a sewing machine. Fold the velvet under 1.3 cm towards the wrong side. You may want to tack this hem so it will be easier to sew to the ribbon. Final finishing involves slipstitching the velvet to the ribbon. Remove the tacking stitches and your stole is ready to wear.

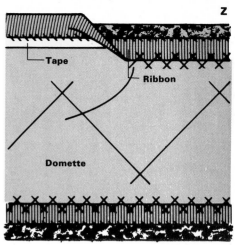

Figure Z: Make rolled hems all around the stole as described for a collar and cuffs (page 40). A small rim of fur shows on the underside.

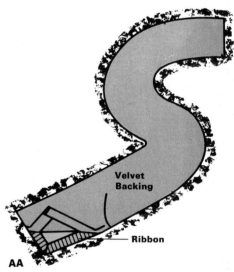

Figure AA: Turn the velvet lining under 1.3 cm and attach it to the ribbon with small slip-stitches. This finishes the stole.

GINGERBREAD

A Baker's Art

By Albert Hadener

Gingerbread is made from a spicy dough traditionally sweetened with honey. It was known to the ancient Egyptians who believed that honey had mystical powers. The first recipe for honey-sweetened cake came from Greece, where it reportedly was devised by a baker on the island of Rhodes about 2400 B.C. As with many things Greek, gingerbread was copied by the Romans and spread throughout their empire. Other European cultures developed their own recipes by adding whatever spices were available. During the early Middle Ages, monks refined the recipes, using newly-acquired exotic spices from the Far East. Thus, today we have many different recipes for gingerbread. Most modern recipes substitute molasses or treacle for honey.

In the 14th, 15th, and 16th centuries, elaborate gingerbread creations became almost an art form in many European countries. Queen Elizabeth I, for example, had bakers create flattering gingerbread likenesses of lords and ladies in her court. Other royalty handed out their own countenances depicted in gingerbread.

Nowhere was gingerbread more closely mixed with culture than in Germany. The German form of gingerbread, known as *lebkuchen*, is a spicy honey cake, and the kind used to make the fairy-tale house opposite. The art of baking *lebkuchen* was so revered during the 14th and 15th centuries in Germany that contests used to be held among bakers from different towns to produce the finest one. The town of Nuremburg often won; its *lebkuchen* is still prized today.

When Grimm wrote *Hansel and Gretel* in the 19th century, the *lebkuchen* house became a German speciality, especially appealing to children.

Kitchen Favourites and Celebrations
Fairy-tale House

An enchanting fairy-tale house like the one pictured on the right is almost as much fun to make as it is to look at—or eat. First cut out cardboard patterns for the pieces as shown on page 45. Prepare dough according to the recipe on page 44, then follow the directions given for cutting and baking. Use the recipe on page 46 to prepare icing for joining the pieces together and decorating. To give the house its fairy-tale appearance, decorate it with bought sweets, and add white icing, marzipan, sweets, hundreds-and-thousands, and almonds. I made Hansel, Gretel, and the witch of marzipan, but you can make them of *lebkuchen* if you prefer. Actual-size patterns for these figures are on page 45.

The total working time needed to make this house is about three or four hours but it is necessary to wait between some stages, so you should spread the work over several days. Plan to prepare and chill the dough one day; roll it out, cut and bake the second day; and assemble and decorate the third day.

Lebkuchen is remarkably sturdy and long-lasting. It will keep indefinitely if not cooked in a pan greased with fat. The recipe on page 44 requires no fat; you bake it on ungreased baking sheets or tins lined with aluminium foil. This means that you can make the house long before Christmas, and keep it even for several years wrapped in plastic and stored in a cool dry place.

The recipe on the next page makes one house plus Hansel, Gretel, and the witch. If you prefer to make *lebkuchen* figures, the same recipe yields about $2\frac{1}{2}$ dozen large "gingerbread boys".

Fairy-tale house, designed by Albert Hadener, is made from *lebkuchen*, a spicy honey-sweetened dough. The decorations are sweets, almonds and snow-like white icing.

Lebkuchen

Recipe ingredients:
850 g honey
225 g sugar
120 ml milk
900 g plain flour
1 tablespoon cinnamon
2 teaspoons each of nutmeg, mace, ground allspice and salt
1 tablespoon baking soda
2 lemon rinds, chopped

Icing:
450 g sifted icing sugar
4 egg whites

Decorations:
almonds
hundreds-and-thousands
handful of small sweets

What you will need

You probably have in your kitchen most of the equipment needed to make the gingerbread house: rolling-pin; pastry board or waxed paper for rolling dough on; 2 large baking sheets (30 by 40 cm) or 4 smaller ones; pastry wheel or paring knife; sugar thermometer; pastry bag with an opening to make a line of icing about 6 mm wide; large mixing bowl; heavy 1 litre saucepan; kitchen scales; measuring spoons. Ingredients (left) are available in any supermarket. To prepare patterns you will need cardboard and scissors.

Making cardboard patterns

Patterns in Figure A on the opposite page are half their actual size. On stiff cardboard, scale up the patterns to the dimensions given and cut them off. Dotted lines on the front pattern show where to cut the front window and door *after* this front section is cut from dough. Dotted lines on the sides show where to place shutters after baking. Those on the chimney pattern show where to cut an angle that fits the slope of the roof. This is done on the chimney front and back *after* baking. Make separate patterns for front door, window shutters, and for Hansel, Gretel, and witch (shown actual size in Figure A).

Preparing the dough

Combine honey, sugar, and milk in a saucepan and heat until the mixture registers 60 to 65° C on a sugar thermometer. While the mixture is heating, mix flour, spices, baking soda and lemon rind in a large bowl.

Pour the hot mixture into the dry ingredients and mix thoroughly. The dough should leave the sides of the bowl and you should be able to shape it into a smooth ball. If it is too wet and sticks, mix in more flour. Chill the dough for two or three hours or overnight in the refrigerator.

1: Cut each piece by laying the cardboard pattern on top of the dough and tracing around it with a pastry wheel or paring knife.

2: Place cut pieces on baking sheets. You can line sheets with aluminium foil or bake on ungreased sheets. Be sure to leave room between pieces for spreading.

3: After the front piece is trimmed, cut the witch's window and front door (see Figure A). Pictured is a round cutter the size of the door opening, but a sharp knife is fine to use.

Rolling and cutting dough

Remove dough from the refrigerator and let it stand until it is soft enough to roll out. (It is easier to divide the dough in quarters and work with one quarter at a time.) Using a lightly floured rolling-pin, roll out the dough on a floured board until it is about 6 mm thick. (You may need to work in more flour.)

Lay cardboard patterns on the dough and cut around them with a pastry wheel or paring knife. Cut a front, a back, two sides, two roof pieces, a base, three chimney pieces and a chimney roof, a front door, and two pairs of shutters. Also cut out Hansel, Gretel, and the witch.

After the front section is cut, follow the dotted lines and cut out the front window and door openings. Cut round windows for both sides. Decorate the arch over the front door by pressing a few almonds into the dough (see photograph, page 43). Press an almond into the front door.

Place cut pieces on ungreased or aluminium foil-lined baking sheets. If you do not have enough baking sheets to accommodate all the pieces, bake several batches. Pieces should be placed about 3 cm apart to allow them to spread.

Continue rolling dough and cutting until you have all the pieces you need.

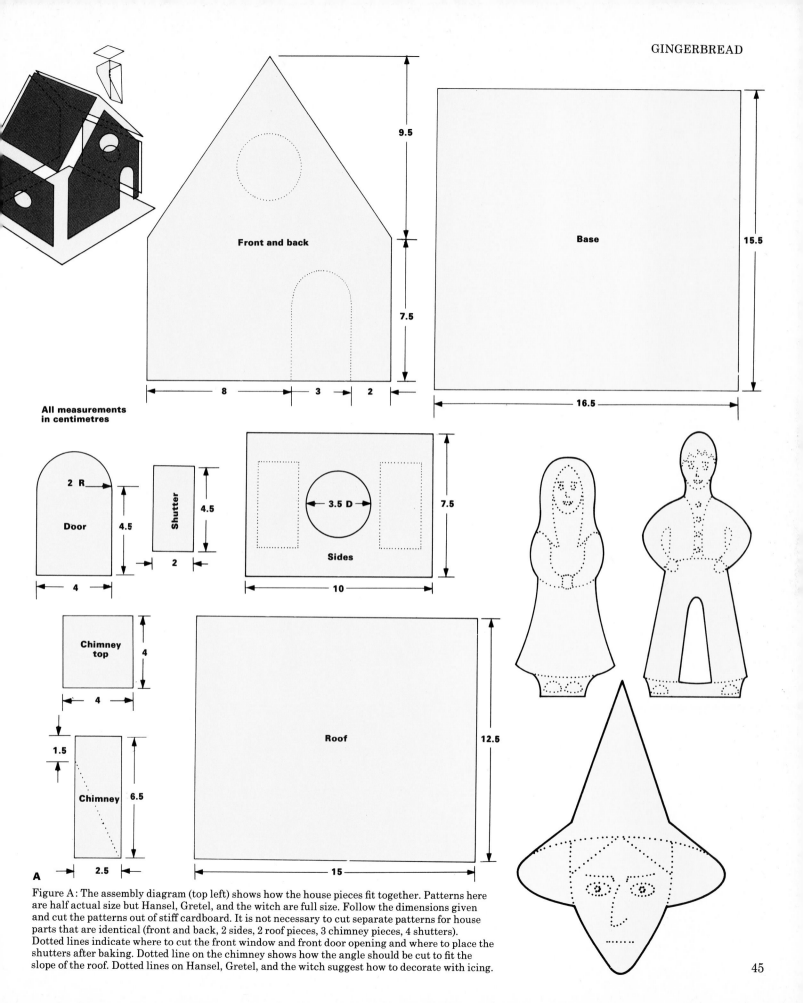

9.5

Front and back

7.5

8   3   2

Base

15.5

16.5

All measurements in centimetres

2 R

Door

4.5

4

Shutter

4.5

2

3.5 D

Sides

7.5

10

Chimney top

4

4

1.5

Chimney

6.5

2.5

Roof

12.5

15

A

Figure A: The assembly diagram (top left) shows how the house pieces fit together. Patterns here are half actual size but Hansel, Gretel, and the witch are full size. Follow the dimensions given and cut the patterns out of stiff cardboard. It is not necessary to cut separate patterns for house parts that are identical (front and back, 2 sides, 2 roof pieces, 3 chimney pieces, 4 shutters). Dotted lines indicate where to cut the front window and front door opening and where to place the shutters after baking. Dotted line on the chimney shows how the angle should be cut to fit the slope of the roof. Dotted lines on Hansel, Gretel, and the witch suggest how to decorate with icing.

Baking

Pre-heat oven to 180° C. Bake for 8 to 10 minutes. Remove *lebkuchen* from the oven and leave on baking sheets until it cools. If you are re-using the baking sheet for additional baking, make sure the sheets cool before starting the next batch. This will prevent dough from spreading.

Icing and assembling

In a large bowl, make the icing by beating 450 g of sifted icing sugar and 4 egg whites until the mixture forms stiff peaks. Place several spoonfuls in a pastry bag fitted with a wide tube opening. (Keep the rest of the icing covered with a damp towel or plastic wrap so it will not dry out.)

Apply a line of icing to the lower outside edge of the back of the house and spread it with a knife to make a 2.5 cm wide band. Dip iced area in coloured hundreds-and-thousands. Apply a line of frosting to the bottom edge (photograph 4). Set the back on the base about 2.5 cm in from the base edge. Hold in place for several minutes until the icing sets.

Cover the shutters with green icing (or any colour you choose). To do this, mix a few spoonfuls of white icing with food colouring in a separate bowl and apply with a knife to cover the shutters. Using icing as an adhesive, attach the shutters beside each side window.

Apply icing to the lower outside edges of the sides and dip them in hundreds-and-thousands. Put the sides in place and hold until set.

4: Put a band of hundreds-and-thousands on the back piece, then apply a line of icing to the bottom so you can affix the back to the base.

5: Reinforce the house corners from inside with an extra line of icing. Then position the witch inside the front window and stick.

6: Gently place joined roof halves on the iced top edges of the house and hold them in place until they set—about five minutes.

7: Attach the chimney and ice roof generously. Place decorations in icing before it hardens. Use the photograph on page 43 as a guide.

Ice and fit the front in place the same way. Then reinforce the joined parts of the house from inside (photograph 5).

With dots of icing, make eyes for the witch. Put some icing on her hat so that you can stick her in place inside the front window. The front door is iced in place after the house is completely assembled.

Take great care when you set the roof on the house so that it does not slip. First, allow front, back, and sides to set undisturbed on the base for about two hours. Meanwhile, ice the roof halves together. To attach the roof, apply icing to the exposed edges of the front, back, and sides. Gently place the roof on the house so it rests evenly (photograph 6). Hold the roof in place and allow to set.

Final decorating

The base of the chimney is cut on the angle shown by the dotted line in Figure A, page 45, so that it will fit the slope of the roof. Cut, then ice the three chimney pieces together and let them set for five minutes. Then ice the chimney to the house. Set the top on the chimney and ice it as well.

Ice the roof with a spatula, using light sweeps to cover the surface liberally. Then position decorations on the roof by pressing them gently into the icing. I used nuts, sweets, marzipan and a foil-wrapped Santa.

You may want to decorate Hansel and Gretel with coloured rather than white icing. Make it by adding food colouring to the remaining white icing. Decorate Hansel and Gretel to your liking and then put them in place. Finally, put the front door in place so that it stands ajar.

Kitchen Favourites and Celebrations
Gingerbread Biscuits

By Lisa Bosboom

The biscuits below were made with traditional gingerbread cutters, available in kitchenware shops and department stores. The smaller figures—the girl with blue skirt (top right) and the two small boys—are traditional European designs. The three large figures—all gingerbread boys—use a popular American design. If you do not want to buy cutters, there are patterns you can enlarge given in Figure B, page 48. Cut cardboard patterns, then trace around them on rolled-out dough with a paring knife.

The recipe for these biscuits calls for molasses, but you can use treacle instead. It makes about two dozen figures.

After biscuits are baked and decorated, wrap them in brightly-coloured tissue paper and place them in baskets or tins.

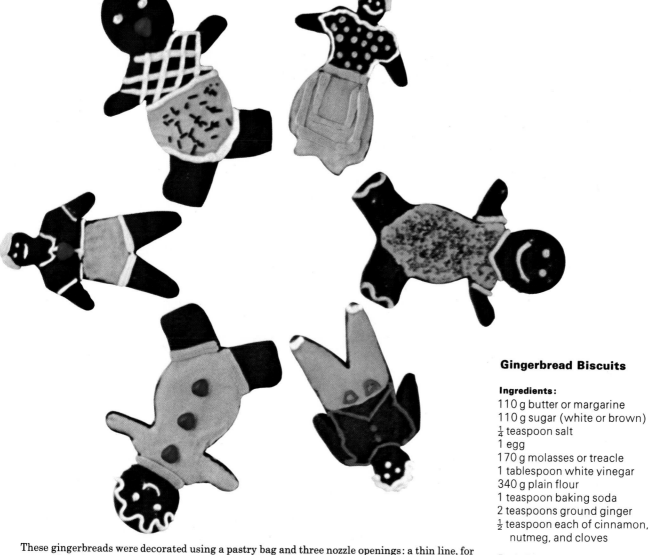

These gingerbreads were decorated using a pastry bag and three nozzle openings: a thin line, for eyes and small details; a thick line for the large boy's lattice top (top left), and thick trims; and a fine stripe for pink apron trim (top right). The same icing can be used for decorating and as a glaze. For elaborate effects, use icing with hundreds-and-thousands and small bits of sweets. Buttons and boy's mouth are heart-shaped sweets.

Gingerbread Biscuits

Ingredients:
110 g butter or margarine
110 g sugar (white or brown)
$\frac{1}{4}$ teaspoon salt
1 egg
170 g molasses or treacle
1 tablespoon white vinegar
340 g plain flour
1 teaspoon baking soda
2 teaspoons ground ginger
$\frac{1}{2}$ teaspoon each of cinnamon,
    nutmeg, and cloves

Basic Icing
300 g sifted icing sugar
$\frac{1}{4}$ teaspoon cream of tartar
2 egg whites

47

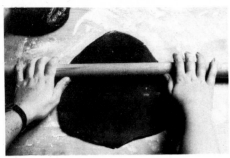

8: Roll out the dough on a lightly floured board using a smooth, firm motion, until it is about 6 mm thick. Add more flour if dough sticks.

9: Cut out shapes. Save scraps to re-roll to make additional biscuits. Excess flour is brushed off before baking.

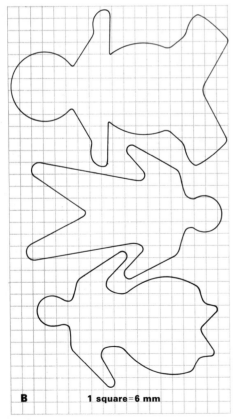

B   1 square = 6 mm

Figure B: To make cardboard patterns, enlarge these patterns on to cardboard, as described opposite in instructions.

How to make gingerbread biscuits

Cream the butter, sugar and salt in a large bowl. Stir in egg, treacle or molasses, and vinegar, and mix well. In another bowl, sift together flour, baking soda, and spices. Add the dry ingredients to the molasses mixture a little at a time and mix thoroughly. Shape the dough into a ball and chill in the refrigerator at least three hours or overnight.

Remove dough from the refrigerator and let it soften. Pre-heat the oven to 190° C. Using a lightly floured rolling-pin, roll out the dough on a floured board until it is about 6 mm thick.

Use cutters to cut out figures or place cardboard patterns on the dough and trace around them with a paring knife. Place them on lightly greased baking sheets. Bake for about 10 minutes. Cool on wire racks for at least a half hour before icing.

Each colourful figure is given an individual look with icing tinted with food colouring. Other combinations of colours and patterns are shown on page 47.

Fun with icing

To make icing, beat 300 g sugar, $\frac{1}{4}$ teaspoon cream of tartar and 2 egg whites until the mixture is so stiff that a knife drawn through it leaves a clean path. You may have to add more sugar to achieve the right consistency. To make coloured icing (photograph, page 47), mix in small amounts of food colouring. Use a separate bowl for each colour.

To use icing as a glaze, thin with a drop or two of hot water. Glaze biscuits first, spreading with a knife. Let glaze harden before adding icing details. Then spot-decorate, using a pastry bag and various tube openings. Experiment with different openings for different effects.

CRAFTNOTES ON ENLARGING PATTERNS

Throughout the volumes of The Family Creative Workshop, patterns are reproduced for you to copy. To make a pattern full size, follow the system described here for enlarging the grid imposed on the heart pattern.

The system is really very simple. The small grid in the book must be translated on to a grid with larger squares that you will make; the design (in this case, the heart) will be copied on to this larger grid. The size of the enlarged grid you make will depend on what the pattern is for. For example, for a pillow pattern the grid will have much smaller squares than will a grid for a tablecloth or a bedspread. A gauge is given with each pattern printed. Draw the squares of the large grid you prepare to the size given by this gauge.

Above is the pattern of a heart as it might appear in these volumes. The grid placed over it is divided into small squares that actually measure 3 mm. All the patterns in the Creative Workshop use grids of this size. To make a pattern to a 6 mm gauge, transfer the heart pattern on to a grid whose squares are 6 mm in size.

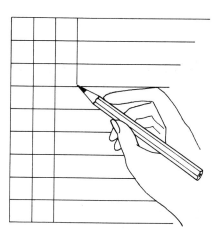

To enlarge the heart pattern, prepare a grid that has the same number of squares as the illustrated grid, but one in which each square measures 6 mm on each side.

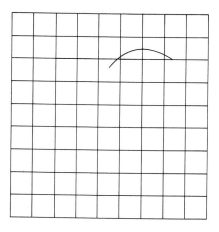

Draw the pattern on to your 6 mm grid, a square at a time.

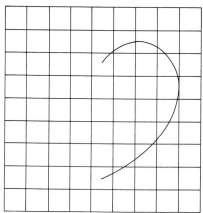

Follow the lines around, checking the book carefully as you draw.

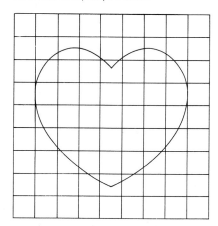

You will find it is easy to transfer the whole pattern using this system.

GLASS WORKING
Forms by Hand and Flame

By Carl H. Betz

What flows like honey one moment, then stands rigid and brittle the next? What has no form of its own, yet takes any and all forms? Thousands of years ago, craftsmen became intrigued with the substance that posed such riddles: glass. Today, the methods of glass working that they evolved are still used in refined forms, as in the simple projects described on pages 52 to 55 and in the more advanced lampwork techniques shown on pages 56 to 63. The small opaque-glass ewer on the right was made by a sand-core technique invented by the ancient Egyptians. This process involved immersing a vessel-shaped mould into a crucible of molten glass. The glass adhering to the mould was then shaped and ornamented. When the glass had cooled, the core was chipped out. This early glass was melted in ceramic crucibles heated with oil lamps, hence the derivation of the term "lampwork" to designate advanced work with glass and flame. In the 1st century A.D., the blowpipe was invented, probably by a Syrian, and the techniques of glass working were revolutionised. That craftsman's method of blowing glass into a mould is still used, but differs from what is now called "off-hand" glass blowing or free-blown glass.

Off-hand glass blowing

Visitors to the famous glass factories throughout the world have seen spectacular demonstrations of off-hand glass blowing. The master glassmaker gathers molten glass from the mouth of the furnace, and blows a magnificent bubble in the air. Crystal goblets, vases and art objects are made by this method; but mass-produced glass is made by machines that reproduce the ancient mould-blowing technique on a grand scale.

Lampwork

Because the heavy metal blowpipes and blazing furnaces were unsuited to the crafting of delicate precision apparatus for laboratory use, a method was devised in the 19th century for using small burners to heat and shape glass. The result was the development of lampwork as a highly skilled craft. Today, lampwork is still used primarily for this purpose, but glass craftsmen are now applying the techniques to the creation of a great variety of art glass objects. Anyone who has taken a chemistry class in school will have bent glass tubes and rods in a small flame. This simple demonstration of the properties of glass is also a good prelude to lampworking, or flameworking, as it is sometimes called.

Kinds of glass

The chemistry of glass deserves study by any glass worker. In simple terms, glass is formed by the fusion of three major oxides (elements that have combined with oxygen to form compounds): silica (sand), or silicon dioxide (SiO_2), is the most important in forming glass, imparting viscosity; soda, or sodium dioxide (NaO_2), speeds fluidity during melting; and lime, or calcium oxide (CaO), sometimes called calcia, adds durability to glass by protecting it against the corrosive effects of water. All of these compounds occur abundantly in nature. Other kinds of oxides (lead is the most widely used, but there are many), when added in varying amounts to the basic combination, produce different kinds of glass varying in hardness, softness, heat resistance and colour (see Craftnotes, page 59). The projects on the following pages use two basically different kinds of glasses, soft and hard. In the first three simple projects, the glass objects are hand-formed rather than blown.

Glass bottles blown by Suellen Fowler (see page 56) demonstrate what can be done with a craftsman's skilled and experienced hand. The balanced forms and subtle colourings result when advanced technique joins imagination, to produce original design variations.

Three thousand years ago, an Egyptian craftsman made this opaque glass ewer, which may have held the perfume and unguents of a queen. It was created during Egypt's 18th dynasty in the reign of Amenhotep II. Decorated with "snake threads" of coloured glass, it is 11.3 cm tall, approximately the size of the contemporary glass bottles opposite.

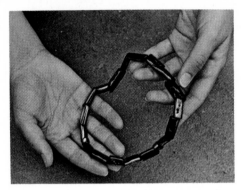

Iridescent grey-blue beads of lead glass can be made quickly and simply even by someone beginning to acquire glass-working skills.

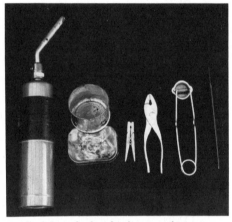

1: All of the soft-glass beginner projects described here can be made with these simple tools: propane torch, tuna fish tin, sardine tin, spring clothes-peg, pliers, spark lighter and three-cornered file.

Glass and Plastics
Creations from Soft Glass

Glasses with a high lead or soda-lime content are called soft because they have a low melting point. Soft glass is also called spun or knit glass and may be used to create small decorative objects. Lead glass tubing, used to make the iridescent beads pictured (left) is the same as that used in neon signs.

Since I have worked most of my life as a master glass maker in research and industry, I am familiar with the properties of all kinds of glasses. Over the years I have developed a special interest in the properties of soft glass and its advantages for the beginning craftsman. First, soft glass will melt in an ordinary propane-torch flame, unlike the hard (Pyrex) glass used for laboratory glassware, which requires a much hotter, oxygen-enriched flame. This means that a beginner can work with glass without needing a complex heat source. Since no special tools are required, the over-all cost is small.

The techniques demonstrated in the three simple projects that follow evolved as the result of an invitation I received, to create an introductory course in glass working for young people at a local arts centre. There were no funds with which to purchase expensive glass-working equipment; and the centre did not wish to ask young students to make a large expenditure for materials. My ingenuity was put to the test and I accepted the challenge. I found that with adequate adult supervision, children between the ages of nine and 13 were able to handle the torch and complete many satisfying projects in soft glass. The time required for each of the soft-glass projects is less than an hour.

Tools, supplies and materials
The few simple tools needed for the projects that follow are pictured (left). The propane torch with a pencil-burner tip (also called hot tip or jet tip), is manufactured under several brand names and is available at almost any ironmonger's or automotive supply shop. I usually work on a table surfaced with laminated plastic. You may wish to take the precaution of covering your work surface with asbestos cement sheet to prevent scorch marks. Plastic safety spectacles should be worn whenever possible.

A supply of soft glass (lead and soda-lime) rods and tubing can be obtained from laboratory equipment suppliers and sign makers listed in the Yellow Pages. Though glass is usually sold by weight, some suppliers prefer to sell small quantities of rods and tubes by length (about 1.50 m). You will need several lengths of 5 mm and 3 mm or 2 mm solid rods (not tubing) of soda-lime glass. One length of 10 mm lead glass tubing will make several of the iridescent necklaces. Lead glass discolours to a luminous blend of grey, blue and gold when heated. Soda-lime glass tubing will not discolour, but you may want to use it to make clear glass beads, and then colour them with lacquer, glass stain (available in hobby shops), or even nail polish. Any glass object can also be sprayed with gold or silver.

Iridescent glass beads
Select a length of 10 mm lead glass tubing. Using the tuna fish tin (photograph 1) and the three-cornered file, break the rod first into more manageable 30 cm lengths, then into bead-sized pieces. Make your first cut by laying the tubing across the top of the notched tin so that it rests in the notch (photograph 2), with 30 cm extending beyond the notch. Place the edge of the file on the tubing above the notch and draw it across, scraping sharply (photograph 3). Rap the tube sharply on the extended end and it will break cleanly (photograph 4). When you have made several 30 cm lengths in this manner, you can make bead-sized pieces (15 to 20 beads for a necklace). The edges of the beads can be made irregular by varying the position of the notched glass on the tin before rapping (photograph 5). If you align the glass notch over the tin notch, the break will be even. By varying the position of the glass notch, either inside or beyond the rim of the tin, you can make the break become irregular, thereby adding variety to the beads.

2: Cut a notch into the rim of the tuna fish tin with a three-cornered file. This will serve as a holder on which to cut rods and tubes.

3: Rest the tubing in the notch and score the glass by drawing the edge of the file sharply across the glass, directly above the notch.

4: Rap the end of the tube good and hard with the three-cornered file. It will break off evenly and cleanly at the tin's rim.

Fractures in individual beads do not mean that the bead must be discarded. So long as the bead is still intact, fractures can be fused in the flame of the torch. When you have cut enough beads for a necklace, ignite the torch with the spark lighter. Do not allow anyone to stand near the flame, do not wear loose clothing, and be sure to direct the flame away from you at all times. Place the sardine tin, bottom side up, on the tuna tin and set one bead on top. Adjust the flame so the inner cone is approximately 2.5 cm high. When you hold the ignited torch upside down, the flame may get larger, so you will have to allow for this when adjusting it. The bead must be heated first on both ends and then in the middle; the point of the inner cone of the flame must touch the glass. The flame is aimed at an angle (photograph 7) so that it penetrates the bead while heating the upper edge of one side to incandescence. When you have fire-polished both ends, bring the tip of the cone down close and direct it steadily at the very centre of the bead (photograph 9) until it becomes incandescent and the colour appears. The tins heat up, so do not touch them with your hands. Take flame away and turn the bead over with the file. It may stick to the surface of the tin but a slight tap with the file will loosen it.

5: These bead-sized pieces have been rapped from 30 cm lengths of glass rod.

Repeat the same firing process on the other side of the bead. The underside of the bead will not melt, as the tin conducts heat away from the glass. For added decoration, you can press the tip of the file into the soft hot glass on one side to make indentations. But if you press too hard, or if you fire-polish the bead too long, the centre will flatten and the bead will not be usable.

As each bead is finished, push it off the sardine tin with the file into an aluminium foil saucer. Give the beads several minutes to cool; then they will be ready to be strung into necklaces like the one pictured opposite, or bracelets. Using thin round elastic eliminates the need for jewellery clasps; the elastic becomes invisible after the knot has been tied and trimmed. Glass beads can also be strung with other kinds of beads—wooden or metal—or added to leather fringe on bags and jackets.

6: Irregular edges and variations in length give an interesting effect in the finished beads.

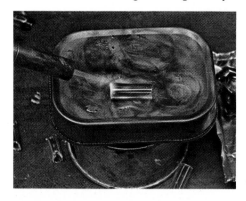

7: Using the bottom of a sardine tin as a work surface, heat the open ends of bead segments, first one and then the other, to incandescence.

8: As you heat the second opening, you will see discolouration begin to transform the bead from clear to a grey-blue-gold iridescence.

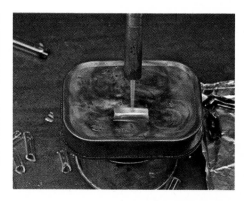

9: To bring out the maximum iridescence of the lead glass, hold the torch steady and direct the flame's cone at the centre of the bead.

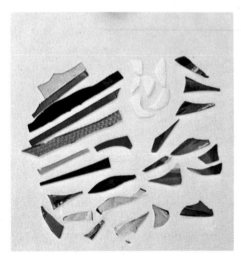

Garnish a glass of lemonade or a cocktail with a hand-made swizzle stick. Colourful tops are made from scraps of bottle and cathedral glass, fused, twisted and swirled in a flame.

Glass and Plastics
Swizzle Sticks

The colourful twisted glass plumes on the swizzle sticks (left) were made from fragments of ordinary bottle and cathedral glass. The rods are 5 mm soda-lime glass. Lead glass is not suggested for this project as the discolouration would not be desirable on swizzle sticks. Scraps of cathedral glass can be bought at hobby shops or you can break up small coloured glass bottles by wrapping them thickly in newspapers and smashing them with a hammer. Do not use large, heavy bottles because large pieces of thick glass might explode in the heat of the flame.

11: Hold a glass fragment and a rod of 5 mm glass in the flame in a V formation and heat both until they start to melt. When both are drippy, press together, remove and straighten.

12: Allow joint to set and return to flame. Heat the first 6 mm of the fragment, turning it back and forth, from edge to edge, until the glass is soft enough to begin the twist.

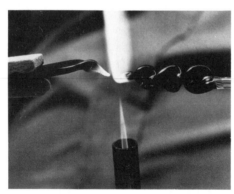

13: When the spiral is about 4 cm long, sever the excess in the flame and fire polish the tip for a final shaping.

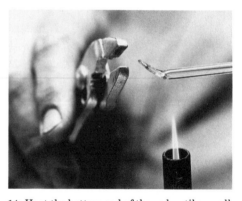

14: Heat the bottom end of the rod until a small glob of glass forms; then squeeze it with pliers and bend it up slightly to form a paddle.

15: To make a flat end, simply press the molten glob on a flat surface, such as the top of the tin.

16: A tear-drop end is formed by rotating the glob at an angle in the flame until it droops.

10: For swizzle sticks, choose glass fragments shaped somewhat like these. Avoid thick shards from large bottles or jugs.

Be careful when selecting fragments as edges and points will be razor-sharp. It is best to pick up the ones you want with a spring-type wooden clothes-peg. Pieces chosen should be wedge-shaped and not less than 5 cm long or 1.5 cm wide. Excess length can be severed easily in the flame. Fragments should not be more than 4 mm thick. Use a clip-type wooden clothes-peg to hold the pieces of glass in the flame. Metal pliers should not be used as the metal would conduct heat away from the glass, causing it to crack.

Attach the fragment to the rod (photographs 11 and 12). Hold the clothes-peg steady and begin the spiral by twisting the rod (photograph 13). After you have severed the excess length put the rod in a tin and let the tip cool in the air. Methods for making three types of bottom ends are described in photographs 14, 15, and 16. In each case, give the end plenty of time to air-cool.

The glass tops need not always be twisted into spirals. If the fragment is an interesting shape, it can simply be attached to the rod and fire-polished.

Glass and Plastics
Form-a-loop Sculpture

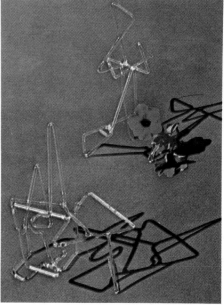

So long as glass and imagination hold out, form-a-loop sculptures like these can be built up into fascinating light-catching forms.

The delicate free-form glass sculptures shown on the right are made from lengths of 2 mm solid glass rod. The basic rules for making form-a-loops are simple: (1) never use hollow tubing of any kind; and (2) except for the first loop (see photograph 18, below), never terminate a loop upon itself, but only upon the one preceding it. You will quickly find that a third hand is necessary if you break the latter rule. Use pieces of rod of uniform lengths to get the best results. Sculptures here were made from 23 cm lengths. Because of the thinness

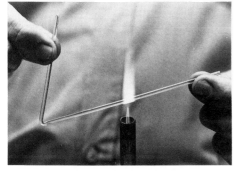

17: The second bend closes the initial triangle. Before bending, rotate the rod in the flame to allow the rod to become equally soft all around.

18: If a bit of rod extends when the triangle is closed, heat it, pull it off with pliers, then fire polish the joint all around.

19: Bend the second loop in the same way as the first, but terminate it on the first loop instead of on itself. Use a clothes peg to help join loops.

of the rod you will be able to use either soda-lime glass (not lead) or borosilicate (Pyrex). But do not try to mix the two, since different types of glass cool at a different rate, causing stresses which make the object crack.

Your first loop is actually a triangle. The bends are made by heating the rod at points that divide the rod into thirds. Allow each bend to cool before proceeding to the next one. After the first bend, you will have a wide V with one leg longer than the other. Bend the long leg back to join the short leg (photograph 17) and fuse the joint in the flame. If a piece of rod extends beyond the joint, trim it off (photograph 18). Turn each joint in the flame so that all sides fuse evenly. Lay the first loop on the table to cool.

The sculpture is made by simply joining loop to loop. Joining the second loop to the first is the only awkward moment. I use a clothes-peg (photograph 19) to help to bend and join the last leg of the second loop to the joint of the first. As you begin to build the sculpture, it actually becomes easier to handle though it looks more and more complex (photograph 20). Finished sculptures may look like humorous abstractions of familiar forms and objects.

20: You can create complex forms by simply attaching and bending rods in all shapes and directions. Mount or suspend sculptures.

Glass and Plastics
Lampblown Glass

By Suellen Fowler

As a lampworker I work on a rather small scale, but I am always aware of the mysteries inherent in this strange, ductile substance from which I coax such endlessly varied forms. Glass offers an almost infinite range of colours, brilliant and subtle, with an unlimited horizon for design.

Lampwork is a highly individual form of glass working, since, unlike off-hand glass blowing, it takes only one person to execute a design. Anyone beginning in lampwork quickly learns to find his own style at his own pace. But a glass craftsman must develop quickness and great manual dexterity before he can claim control of his unusual medium.

Costs and supplies

While costs may vary, a basic set of equipment and tools can be obtained for £100 to £150. (Jencons Scientific Ltd. of Hemel Hempstead, Herts., among others, can supply both equipment and borosilicate (Pyrex type) tubing and rod.) Apart from hand tools you will need a torch and holder (Jencons "Flair" or "Jet 7"), oxygen regulator and, unless using piped gas supplies, a fuel gas regulator (from British Oxygen Corporation, who can also supply the oxygen and fuel gas), a hose set, and protective goggles. A supply of 5 mm and 13 mm rod and 15 mm heavy wall tubing will suffice for beginners.

A suitable workspace

A garage or shed with good ventilation, but free from draughts, away from the house, is an ideal space for lampwork (especially since the tanks of oxygen and fuel-gas that feed the blowtorch should be kept out of doors). This is not a craft to be practised in a flat or in any cramped space where leaking gases could possibly accumulate.

Before you set up any kind of glass workshop, ask your local council about fire precautions and gas storage regulations. Also make a careful check of your household insurance policy. Never let children gain access to any equipment or work areas.

I work in a shed on a sturdy old wooden table, large enough to accommodate my blowpipe, tools, and several lengths of tubes and rods. The table's surface has become covered with char marks. But the danger of igniting the table is small, since the blowtorch is always secured in a stationary position by its holder (Figure A), and hot glass is not hot enough to ignite wood. To be on the safe side, many lampworkers use asbestos cement sheeting.

This lampblown perfume bottle and stopper demonstrates the lovely symmetry that can be achieved with the glass blower's art.

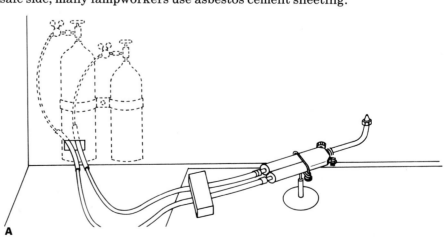

A

Figure A: A set-up to deliver oxygenated fuel gas to a glass-working shop is shown. For safety's sake, the blowtorch is fixed in place on the workbench. Each tank has its own pressure regulator. Copper tubing carries the gases through the wall of the workshop.

One of the major hazards in any work area is clutter, so banish all rags, papers and other free-floating debris to the rubbish bin immediately. Never wear floppy clothes that might inhibit the movement of arms and hands or swing into the flame, or any fabric known to be especially inflammable. And have a fire extinguisher on hand at all times.

Oxygen-fuel gas equipment

The borosilicate glass used by lampworkers has a high melting point. To create a flame with enough concentrated heat to melt this glass, fuels such as natural gas or liquefied petroleum gases (propane or butane) must be burned in the presence of oxygen. When the fuel gas and oxygen are fed simultaneously into the blowtorch, an extremely hot, oxygen-enriched flame is produced. Both the oxygen tank and the fuel gas tank are pressurized and must be used with regulators. Manufacturers provide excellent instructions for attaching such regulators and the connecting hoses.

Lighting the blowtorch

Didymium spectacles shield my eyes from the glaring yellow flare-off that occurs during the interaction between flame and glass. Failure to use these can result in damaged vision, especially when making coloured glass (Craftnotes, page 59) for which welding goggles are even better. I put them on before lighting the blowtorch, which comes fully assembled from the manufacturer, but the oxygen tip must be selected and attached.

I adjust the oxygen pressure to between 2.25 and 3.18 kilos, and the gas pressure to between 1 and 1.8 kilos at the most. To light the torch, I first turn the red (gas) knob on the torch one half-turn anti-clockwise and ignite it with a spark lighter. The pure gas flame is yellow. As the oxygen is added, it turns the flame blue. I turn the oxygen (green) knob slowly clockwise until a steady, light blue inner cone, 1.5 to 2 cm high, is achieved. The outer dark blue flame is 15 to 18 cm high. To turn off the torch, I switch the oxygen off first, then the gas. Both are turned off at the tank source if I stop work for more than 10 minutes. Using oxygen with natural or coal gas, as more oxygen is fed into the jet the inner cone becomes smaller and the heat more intense. The blowtorch tip is constructed so that it directs the flame up and away from me at a slight angle (Figure A). From time to time, I must adjust the flame, however, making it either smaller and more of a pinpoint for heating tiny areas, or larger when an entire object needs to be warmed, for example.

Making a blowpipe

When I made my own blowpipe for the first time from a piece of 1.5 cm tubing, I learned some basic things about the properties of borosilicate glass. The molten glass has the consistency and flow of cold, thick honey. Because glass is a poor conductor (and, conversely, a good insulator) of heat, only the part that is held in the flame melts. It is possible for me to hold a glass rod or tube in my fingers at one end while heating it at the other with no fear of burning myself. An object that has been heated, however, retains heat long after it loses its incandescence, from 10 minutes to half-an-hour or even longer.

What keeps the molten glass from drooping down into an unworkable mass? The answer is rotation, a basic technique requiring much dexterity—but one that must be mastered by a lampworker to ensure the successful forming of his objects. (It often takes months for a lampworker or off-hand glass blower to learn how to rotate the blowpipe while blowing a perfectly rounded bubble.)

Glass must be rotated steadily in the flame to melt and fuse thoroughly and counteract the downward pull of gravity. As a beginner, I found it difficult to melt and fuse because my rotation technique was jerky. But gradually, as I became familiar with and could anticipate the melt and flow, I gained confidence and a steadier hand. I practised first with a piece of 1.5 cm tubing, holding it horizontally between thumbs and fingertips. The thumbs roll it up and over alternately, one beginning where the other leaves off so a continuous rotation cycle is maintained. The tube is severed in the middle by

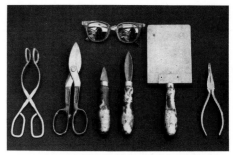

21: Small hand tools used by a lampworker include, left to right: metal tongs, shears, small brass flaring tool and larger flaring tools used to shape openings, marver (also called a carbon flat) used as a levelling surface, small-nosed pliers; top, Didymium protective glasses.

An old engraving shows the proud stance of an off-hand glass blower. His craft links him with ancient Egyptian and Syrian craftsmen.

22: The central portion of a piece of 1.5 cm Pyrex tubing is rotated and pulled apart in the flame as the first step in making a blowpipe.

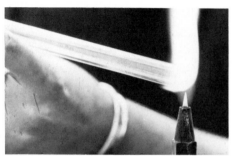

23: The mouthpiece is fire polished by rotating it in the flame until the rough edges melt. It is then pressed and evened on the marver.

24: To start a basic bubble, a wrap of 5mm rod is coiled around the blowpipe. The flame does not touch the blowpipe wall but heats only the small area of rod being coiled.

25: The bubble is ready to be blown when it is whitish-pink as seen through Didymium lenses. Hanging the tube between thumb, index and ring finger, the bubble is blown out, but never while the glass is in the flame.

being rotated just above the inner blue cone of the flame (photograph 22). As a general rule, if the glass starts to droop I know I am rotating it too slowly; if it becomes lopsided, I am not rotating at an even rate. The glass becomes incandescent and melts in about 30 seconds. As the centre melts, I pull the tube apart. The melted glass on both ends contracts back into the tubes and fuses the ends closed. I now have made two blowpipes, each about 60 cm long. Next, I smooth, by fire polishing, the open end of one of the blowpipes (photograph 23), being careful not to close the opening with too much polishing. The blowpipe is ready as soon as open mouthpiece has cooled.

The basic bubble

In lampwork, a part of the blowpipe itself, the first 4 cm of the closed end, becomes part of the basic bubble. Because the walls of the blowpipe are quite thin, however, there is not enough glass in that first 4 cm to be melted and blown into a completed bubble, so extra glass must be added to the outer wall. When this is done the glass will be of sufficient thickness to be heated and blown. It is impossible for molten glass to fuse with cold glass, so all pieces that are to be joined must first be warmed briefly in the flame. First I cut a piece of 5 mm rod in half in the flame, like the blowpipe tubing. Then I warm the sealed end of the blowpipe in the flame, heat the tip of the 5mm rod, and touch rod to tubing about 4 cm from the end. The rod will attach itself to the warmed tubing. With one hand I hold the blowpipe next to but just outside the flame, so it will not melt. I heat the rod just in front of the point of joining and begin to turn the blowpipe slowly, feeding the rod in with the other hand (photograph 24). When the rod has been coiled all the way to the tip of the blowpipe, I sever it with the flame and pull it off. It is important never to force glass for fear of needlessly cracking it during a crucial stage of work. If a coil is not going on smoothly and I have to tug on it, the glass is not hot enough.

Blowing out the bubble

Holding the blowpipe horizontally in both hands (photograph 29 on page 60), I introduce the tip of the coils into the flame and rotate the tubing until the coils melt and fuse. Continuing to rotate the blowpipe, I gradually introduce more of the unmelted coils until they are all melted and fused into each other. The fused tip is then taken out of the flame and held vertically with the bubble hanging down (photograph 30, page 61). Next I blow it out gently to a diameter of about 4 cm. I hold the suspended bubble in this position until it sets (about 30 seconds), then I rest it gently on the marver to cool. Only after this technique of forming a symmetrically-shaped bubble is mastered can a glass worker attempt other projects

Annealing; stopping and restarting

In lampwork, because the pieces we work with are small and the wall of the bubble fairly thin, the annealing (tempering) process is much shorter than it would be for large-scale, off-hand glass blowing. Still, all glass is subjected to a great deal of stress during the cooling process. This occurs because the outer wall of the bubble cools and contracts more quickly than the inner wall where the heat is more confined. Because of its chemical composition, borosilicate glass is able to withstand more extreme cooling stresses than soft glass. Small pieces, like a bead or Christmas ornament (page 63), are allowed to air-cool on the marver, while a bottle must be buried in vermiculite as it cools (page 61) to slow the annealing process. Before laying a piece down to cool, however, I make sure it has lost its incandescence, and has air-cooled for at least 30 seconds. Then I turn off the oxygen and rotate it in the yellow gas flame for a few seconds to bring the temperature down gradually.

To continue working on a halted piece, I turn on the gas flame and rotate the piece in the yellow flame for two or three minutes until it is blackened with carbon. Then I turn on the oxygen slowly to make the flame hotter and proceed with the project. This ensures an even rise in temperature throughout the piece I am working on and keeps the glass from cracking because it has contracted or expanded too rapidly in one spot. Once a blown piece has cracked, it is impossible to fix it.

Reinforcing the basic bubble

To make a glass bottle, additional coils of coloured glass (see Craftnotes below) must be wound on to the basic bubble. But even before adding these coloured coils, I reinforce the neck of the basic bubble by laying on short strips of 5mm rod at intervals around the blowpipe. The reinforcement supports the weight of added coils. Figure B, below, illustrates in three steps the methods I use to add these strengthening strips.

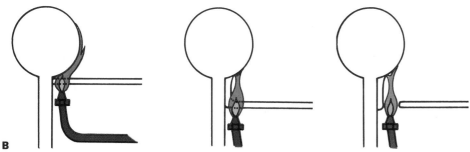

B

Figure B: The neck of the basic bubble is reinforced by first heating the tip of a 5 mm rod and attaching it to the base of the bubble. The rod is then drawn through the flame and fused along 1.5 cm of blowpipe. The rod is severed by pulling off through the flame.

CRAFTNOTES: MAKING COLOURED GLASS RODS

Lampblown objects are coloured by means of coloured glass rods that are made by the glass blower. It is difficult, and sometimes impossible, to find coloured borosilicate rods ready-made. I can experiment with variations in colour by mixing the oxides as I please. The colouring agents are various metallic oxides that come in powder form and can be purchased by weight at ceramic and scientific supply outlets. Cobalt oxide makes a deep blue; tin oxide makes milk-white; chromium oxide makes green; copper oxide makes red. Silver oxide makes yellow, but this is often difficult to obtain except from chemical suppliers. Pastel colours are achieved by combining three parts of one oxide, such as cobalt, with one part tin oxide. Many oxides are toxic, so ensure good ventilation, avoid inhaling fumes, and wash hands thoroughly after using oxides.

To make a blue rod, I start by cutting a 10 cm section of 1.5 cm tubing in the flame, as in making a blowpipe. If both ends seal, I crack one end to let the air escape. Then I attach a 30 cm piece of 1.5 cm rod, reserving one more piece of rod of the same length. As shown above, I place ⅛ teaspoon of cobalt oxide in the

tubing; then I attach a second piece of 1.5 cm rod on to the bottom lip of the open end, leaving a space for air to escape while the tube is being heated.

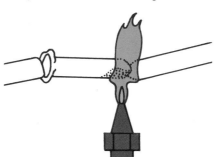

Holding the tube by the rods on either side, I heat the 10 cm tube segment until it softens (above), then I collapse the tube inwards, pushing and kneading the glass into a ball with the rods. I twist and turn the glass ball in the flame to mix the oxide with the molten glass.

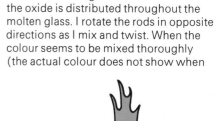

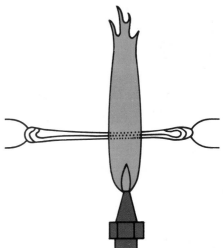

I continue mixing as shown above until the oxide is distributed throughout the molten glass. I rotate the rods in opposite directions as I mix and twist. When the colour seems to be mixed thoroughly (the actual colour does not show when the glass is incandescent), I take the ball out of the flame and begin to pull the mixing rods slowly apart, drawing the glass into a thin 2 or 3 mm rod about 30 cm long. Then I detach one mixing rod from the end of the coloured stick by severing it in the flame and hold the coloured rod with pliers to detach the other rod in the same way. To make the blue glass bottle on page 56, I used two dark blue rods and one light blue rod.

A second wrap of coloured coils

Using the light and dark cobalt blue rods, the second wrap of coils is now added. I turn up the oxygen about a quarter turn to produce a very hot flame and use this to warm the bubble. Then I warm the tip of a light blue rod and begin to coil it around the bubble, starting at the base and winding continuously three times around. The rings are overlapped slightly to prevent gaps in colour. I lay two dark blue coils next to the light blue ones, then finish covering the bubble in the same way coiling on more light blue rods to the tip. The coils are fused and blown out a little.

26: The second wrap of light blue coils is started at the base of the bubble, just above the reinforcements that were added to the neck.

27: At the halfway point, the light blue rod is severed and two coils of dark blue are added; then the rest is covered with light blue coils.

28: A blue rod is used to "comb" the coloured coils into a scallop design around the neck of the bubble before the coils are fused together.

29: The artist demonstrates the hand positions she uses for rotating the blowpipe when she is fusing the coils in the flame.

Combing a design

To shape the design, the coils must be combed while they are still soft and warm, so it is essential that I work quickly at this point. To avoid distortion of the bubble, I adjust the flame to a pinpoint that will heat only a small area at one time. I select a blue rod, heat the tip, and catch it on the bubble's side at the edge of the dark rings. Next I drag, or comb, the hot glass down (photograph 28), in a straight line to the neck of the bubble. The flame heats only the point where the tip of the rod and the coils touch. As I do this, I make the rings describe a continuous scallop design around the neck of the bubble.

When the scallop is completed, I pull the combing rod off in the flame. If a small knob of glass is left on the bubble, I can remove it by heating the knob, taking the bubble out of the flame and, with small-nosed pliers, pulling the knob off. Now the coils are ready to be fused. The flame is turned up again to 15 to 18 cm. Holding the blowpipe in both hands again (as in making the basic bubble), I put the coils in the flame and fuse them (photograph 29), rotating steadily. Smooth fusion depends upon good heat and smooth rotation, not on the way the coils are wrapped. Minor irregularities in the coloured rods or overlapping in the coiling will be fused smooth when rotated in the flame.

Drooping the neck of the bottle

When the coils have fused, I stand and raise the blowpipe to a 45-degree angle to the flame. The mouthpiece is the high end and the bubble is in the flame. The flame is concentrated just below the upper third of the bubble. When rotated in this position, the neck of the bottle begins to elongate and droop. The moment this begins to happen, I remove the bubble from the flame and hold it vertically (photograph 30), until the neck straightens and sets. The body of the bubble is then re-warmed in the flame, removed, and blown out to its final shape and size: approximately 6.5 cm high by 7.5 cm wide. (Blowing is done only when the glass is *not* in the flame.) I give the bottle a flat base by pressing it gently on to the surface of the marver, anneal it in a yellow gas flame for a few moments, then push it into a bucket of vermiculite (photograph 31) to cool.

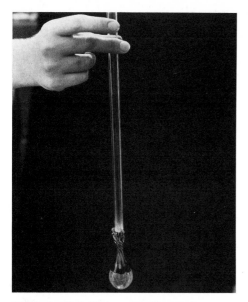

30: The bottle is blown out to its actual finished size as the blowpipe is held in a vertical position between thumb and two fingers.

31: With the blowpipe still attached, the bottle is buried in a bucket of vermiculite, where it is left to cool for several hours.

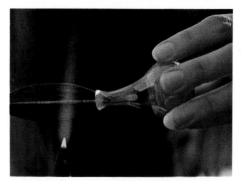

34: A flaring tool is inserted into the neck and turned gently. If the lip will not flare, the glass is too cool and needs still more heating.

32: The bottle is severed from the blowpipe in the flame just below the reinforced area and pulled off with a sealed end in the flame.

33: The sealed tip of the bottle is cracked off with small-nosed pliers. The edges left will be jagged, so the open tip is re-heated in the flame.

35: After the mouth of the bottle has been flared to the desired size, it is pressed gently on the marver and evened.

The mouth of the bottle and stopper

When the bottle has cooled to air temperature, I sever it from the blowpipe using the flame to make a mouth and lip, as shown in photographs 32 to 35.

The first step in making the glass stopper is, again, much the same as making a basic bubble. The tip of a piece of 1.5 cm clear, solid rod (not tubing) is wrapped with 6 mm of cobalt blue coils. The coiled tip is then rotated in the flame and fused into a ball. When fused, the ball is removed from the flame and the heated end held down vertically until it sets. The tip of any easily handled length of 5 mm rod is then heated and joined to the top of this ball. As the 1.5 cm rod is held vertically, the 5 mm rod will align and set. This rod serves temporarily as a handle. This method is often used instead of pliers when working with small pieces (beads, Figure C, page 62).

The section of 1.5 cm rod (photograph 36) just below the ball is rotated in the flame until soft. It is then taken out of the flame and held vertically so the 1.5 cm rod, blue ball and 5 mm rod are all in alignment. The 5 mm rod is pulled gently downwards, causing the stopper's tail to be pulled out of the clear rod.

At this point, the blue ball is about 2.5 cm long and 2 cm around; the tail is about 3 mm wide and 2.5 cm long. When the tail has set, the 5 mm rod is severed in the flame and pulled off. The knob is then rotated and fire polished in the flame. Then I take it out of the flame, hold it ball-downwards, and let it set. I hold the ball with tongs and sever the tail in the flame. The completed stopper is held in the tongs for a moment, just long enough to let the delicate tail set. It can then be placed on the marver to cool.

36: Before the stopper's tail is pulled out, the 1.5 cm rod is heated at the point where it extends from the ball.

61

You would smile too if wearing these multi-coloured hand-blown glass beads.

Glass and Plastics
Glass Beads

The blue glass bead pictured below was made by using the basic bubble technique as a starting point. Any of the coloured glass rods could be used to vary this design. I begin by warming the sealed end of my blowpipe and the tip of a coloured rod at the same time. Starting 1.5 cm from the blowpipe tip. I wind on coloured coils until they reach the tip. I sever the coloured rod in the flame, then rotate and fuse the coils (photograph 29, page 60). When coils have fused, I remove the tip from the flame and blow gently to form an elongated bubble, approximately 1.5 cm long and 6 mm in diameter. The tip of the bubble is then heated again (photograph 37). When it is hot, I remove it quickly from the flame and blow hard into the pipe. This creates a thin-shelled bubble (photograph 38). I knock this bubble gently on a hard surface to break it off. A

37: The extreme tip of the bead bubble is heated to incandescence in the flame.

38: By blowing into the pipe hard and quickly after heating the tip, this thin-shelled, easily-shattered bubble is produced, then cracked off.

39: Shears are used to trim the jagged edge of the broken bubble, leaving a bead to be finished by flaring, marvering and fire-polishing.

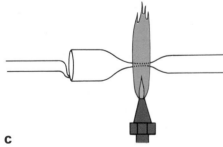

C

Figure C: A 5 mm rod, attached to a bit of the bead lip, serves as a handle for pulling the bead from the blowpipe.

40: In this blue bead, the white stripe has been combed (see page 60) into a scallop design.

rough edge results, which I trim off with shears (photograph 39), then flare slightly and press gently on the marver. To remove the bead from the blowpipe, I attach a handle of 5 mm rod to one part of the finished bead lip (Figure C). This I do exactly the same way as for the bottle stopper (page 61). When this rod has set, I heat the blowpipe just below the blown-out bead and pull the bead out of but not off the pipe, using the 5 mm rod as a handle. I then sever the bead from the pipe in the flame, leaving a sealed end, as was done with the neck of the bottle (photograph 32, page 61). I crack the sealed end off the bead with pliers and finish the opening by heating, trimming, flaring and marvering as I did the other side. Still holding it by the rod, I let it set. The rod is removed by holding the bead with pliers and heating the spot where it joins the bead lip in a small needlepoint flame. The rod can then be severed and pulled off. If a glob of glass is left on the bead lip, the spot can be melted off by fire-polishing. The finished bead is placed on the marver to cool.

Design variations
Bead designs can be varied by coiling several colours on one bead, by varying the combing technique to create more irregular lines, or by adding hobnails of contrasting colour to a finished bead. I also love to experiment by varying the sizes of the beads although the shapes are always slightly irregular.

Glass and Plastics
Hanging Ornament

To create ornaments like the one on the right, I begin once again with the basic bubble. I reinforce the neck and enlarge the bubble with a second wrap of coils. Using any combination of coloured rods, I lay stripes of glass radiating from the tip of the bubble to 2.5 cm along the neck of the blowpipe. I turn the torch down to a small pinpoint flame, warming the bubble and 2.5 cm of neck tubing, select a coloured rod, heat the tip, and attach it to the tip of the bubble (photograph 41). As I heat the section of rod just ahead of the part that has been attached, I curve it around the bubble and down to the neck and along 2.5 cm of tubing. I lay on three more stripes at quarter turns around the bubble in the same way, then rotate and fuse the stripes in the flame but leave the neck stripes unfused, in relief. Holding the blowpipe horizontally (photograph 42), I blow the bubble out to a diameter of about 7.5 cm. When the bubble is blown in this position instead of downwards, I must blow and rotate the blowpipe at the same time maintaining an even rhythm. The result is a less pear-shaped and more rounded bubble. It requires practice and co-ordination to keep the pull of gravity from distorting the bubble. I allow the bubble to set, then attach a piece of 5 mm rod, about 15 cm long, to the top of the bubble and allow this rod to set in line with the blowpipe. Then, holding the bubble in the flame by tube and rod, I rotate the striped neck of the bubble until it softens. Then I take it out of the flame, hold it vertically by the blowpipe, and pull down gently on the rod, pulling out the ornament's neck to about 5 cm but leaving it attached to the blowpipe. Then I allow the neck to set.

The corkscrew tail and hook
I next adjust the flame so the cone is about 6 mm high, and heat the point where the rod joins the bubble. Holding the blowpipe in my right hand, I bend the rod at a 90-degree angle to the blowpipe; then, with the rod in my left hand, I slowly turn the blowpipe away from me, drawing the rod into a corkscrew tail (photograph 43), continuously heating the rod just ahead of the section being curled. The corkscrew is 7.5 to 10 cm long. Next, I straighten the uncurled portion of rod at the base of the corkscrew by warming the bend and hanging it down between my fingers. It re-sets in line with the blowpipe once again.

Now I sever the blowpipe from the ornament. The technique is basically the same one I used to sever the neck of the bottle from the blowpipe (page 61, photograph 32). I hold the ornament by the straightened piece of rod at the end of the corkscrew tail and put the base of the pulled-out neck in the flame, then sever the neck in the flame with a sealed tip. I snip off the tip of the sealed tubing with pliers, fire-polish the open tip without closing the hole; then heat and attach another 5 mm rod to the open end, sealing it again. I heat and bend this rod into a C-curved hook, then sever the rod from hook in the flame.

Holding the body of the ornament with tongs, I sever the straightened end of the corkscrew in the flame and place ornament on the marver to cool.

41: A coloured rod is attached to the tip of the warmed bubble then wrapped around and down along 2.5 cm of the neck of the blowpipe.

42: A bubble blown and rotated simultaneously in this position is more rounded than the pear-shaped vertically-blown bubble.

43: A rod attached to the tip of the bubble is heated just ahead of the part being coiled, beginning the corkscrew.

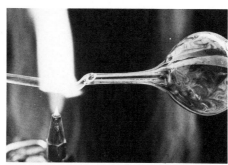

44: A hook is formed by bending a second piece of 5 mm rod attached at the blowpipe end and severing it in the flame.

The finished ornament is ready to hang in a sunny window or on a Christmas tree.

GOLD LEAFING
Much from Little

By Walter Methner

Hammering gold into a thin layer of leaf to make a little of the precious metal go a long way is an age-old art. More than 25 centuries ago, the Greek poet Homer mentioned the beating of gold into thin sheets, and in ancient Egypt, the mummified remains of Pharaohs were entombed in gold-leafed cases.

From those early times until this century, artisans hammered gold into leaf by hand. Now, gold is beaten by machine into sheets 8.5 cm square and less than .0001 mm thick. Gold leaf is so thin that 28g contains enough to cover a 16 to 18 sq. m surface area.

Suitable surfaces

You can apply gold leaf to almost any smooth, hard, non-porous surface—painted or varnished wood, for example, or glass. There are also paints, pastes and powders that simulate gold, but none of these have its brilliance or its resistance to tarnish, although they are less expensive.

Even though the gold substitutes do not contain real gold, they are included in the broad meaning of the term "gilding". However, gold leafing means one thing only: the covering of a surface such as a mirror frame or a chair, with gossamer-thin sheets of real gold.

Candidates for gold leafing

Gold leaf, which can be used in a number of ways, is particularly effective in gilding furniture. The chair shown here was gold-leafed to accentuate the carving on the back; and the method used (see page 68) can be applied to many furnishings, including picture or mirror frames. Gold leaf is also widely used for lettering signs—you can see gold signs in almost any business district on shop windows, in offices and even on van panels. If you wish to make a gold-leafed sign of your own, see the instructions on page 71.

Like shop windows, glassware can be gilded with leaf. Instructions for this and other projects follow.

An inexpensive experiment

For experimenting with the way gold leaf looks and to get used to some of the techniques, you may want to use an imitation called composition leaf or Schlag leaf. This is an inexpensive alloy of copper and nickel which resembles gold, but will tarnish quickly unless it has a protective coating of varnish. I chose composition leaf to gild the outer edges of a shadow box (page 66) because it is an easy, inexpensive way to start working with leaf.

Kinds of gold leaf

Gold leaf is packed in cardboard folders called books. Each of the 25 leaves in a book is separated from its neighbour by a sheet of tissue paper. If the tissue and leaf are packed loosely together, the gold is called loose gold or loose leaf. This type of gold should be used for the chair (page 68) and the dish (page 69). If each sheet of gold is adhered to a sheet of tissue paper, it is called transfer leaf or gilding gold. This, used on the sign (page 72), is not quite as shiny as loose gold, but it is easier to handle because the tissue reinforces the material until it is applied to a surface and the tissue removed.

A microscopically thin layer of 23-carat gold leaf accentuates the carving on the back of the chair (opposite) with a lustre that cannot be achieved with gold-like paints, pastes or powders.

Loose gold leaf is sold in two grades, surface gold and glass gold. Glass gold has fewer imperfections than surface gold and costs slightly more. It is so named because sign painters use it for gilding glass, where pinholes or other flaws would be particularly noticeable. Both types, however, can be applied to any suitable surface with equal ease. The wooden chair (page 68) and the glass dish (page 69) were both gilded with glass gold.

The adhesive that holds the gold leaf to a surface is called gold size. There are several types of size, but for the projects here you will need only two, quick gold size, for the chair, sign and shadow box, and water size for the glass dish. You can purchase quick gold size ready made (see sources listed below), but water size must be mixed fresh for each use by dissolving a gelatine capsule (available from gilding suppliers) in hot water (see page 70).

An array of brushes

Gilding requires an assortment of brushes. You will need one known as a gilding tip to pick up the fragile leaves of loose gold and lay them on the prepared surface. This brush—once fashioned from the tip of a squirrel's tail—is now made by mounting a broad, thin row of camel-hair bristles between two pieces of cardboard. Its use is explained on page 70. You will also need a 5 to 7.5 cm wide household paint brush, for applying water size, and several camel-hair or sable artist's brushes. These should include a No. 8 and No. 16 flat and a No. 2 and No. 12 round for coating smaller areas with size or varnish. When deciding which brush to use, choose the largest practical for the area you are coating. When lettering, for example, you would want one slightly narrower than the narrowest line. You may also want to try a French quill—a brush widely used by sign painters for lettering and striping which has a long round tip of camel or greyhound hair. Another aid is a mahlstick that you can use to steady your hand when lettering or doing other fine work (see photograph 14, page 73). Other materials you will need are listed with each project. Sources of materials are given below.

Where to find supplies

Some gilding materials are available at large painting and decorating shops as well as sign-painting supply houses that may be listed in the Yellow Pages of your telephone directory. All kinds of gold leaf which are used here, and materials for gilding, are obtainable by mail order from George M. Whiley Ltd., Victoria Road, Ruislip, Middlesex.

Furniture and Finishes
Gilt-edge Shadow Box

Gilding the outside edges of a shadow box (see photograph, left) creates a bright frame for the objects displayed in the box's compartments.

I chose composition leaf (see page 64) for the shadow box because it costs less than genuine gold leaf and makes this project an inexpensive introduction to the art of applying leaf to a surface.

Materials needed

In addition to the shadow box, you will need one book of composition leaf; 60 g of quick gold size; yellow (lemon oil-base) pigment; a flat camel-hair brush, slightly narrower than the rim of the box; a roll of absorbent cotton wool; fine sandpaper; clear, glossy polyurethane varnish; and solvents for the varnish and gold size. (Different manufacturers recommend different solvents; see the labels on the containers.)

Work in a well ventilated room, not centrally heated, that is free from draughts and dust. Dust can spoil a gilding job, and the vapours of some solvents, varnishes and sizes can make you feel ill if you are exposed to them for too long a period.

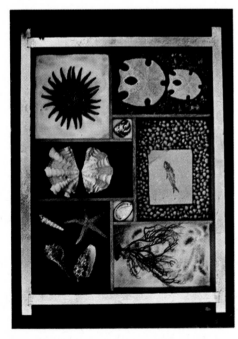

The gilt edging framing the objects in this shadow box was created by applying imitation gold leaf to the rim. This is an easy, low-cost way to familiarise yourself with gilding.

Preparing the box

I started the shadow box by removing one side, sliding out the glass, replacing the side and smoothing the face of the rim with fine sandpaper. Then I painted the sanded edge with two coats of polyurethane varnish. If the shadow box you are gilding has already been finished, sand and varnish the face of the edge anyway to be certain that it is smooth and non-porous.

When the last coat of varnish has dried—allow at least a week for this to make sure any trace of tackiness has disappeared—sand the surface lightly with fine sandpaper (photograph 1) and wipe it free from dust with a rag moistened with the varnish solvent.

Sizing the edge

Mix quick gold size with 1½ teaspoons of yellow pigment. The pigment makes the size easy to see so you will know where you have painted, and a light rather than a dark surface beneath the leaf adds brilliance to the leaf.

Paint the edge of the box with size, covering only the area you want to gild. The leaf will follow the size exactly: If you miss an area with the size, you will have a bare spot when you lay on the leaf. If the size runs over an edge, so will the leaf. The size will take from 1 to 2 hours to set. While you are waiting, use scissors to cut the leaf into strips about 6 mm wider than the width of the edge you intend to gild. Do not peel off the tissue backing that adheres to each leaf. This will be removed later.

Testing the size

Start testing the size about 20 minutes after you apply it. Making sure your hands are clean, touch the knuckle of your first finger to the size. If the size is ready for gilding, it will feel dry to the touch, but you will feel a slight suction when you pull your hand away.

1: Smooth varnished edge of shadow box with fine sandpaper. Wipe away any dust with a rag moistened with varnish solvent and paint the edge with quick gold size.

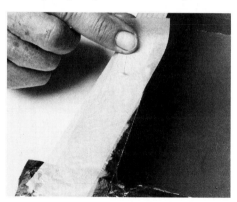

2: Lay strips of composition leaf on the edge so that each strip overlaps the previous strip by at least 3 mm. Remove tissue from each strip of leaf after it is in place.

3: Strike the leaf firmly with the edge of your hand to smooth it into the size. This will also knock away some excess leaf. The rest will tear away when you polish it with cotton wool.

Laying the leaf

When the "knuckle test" indicates that the size is ready, pick up a strip of leaf by the tissue attached to it and lay the exposed leaf along the edge of the box, so that the leaf extends over the edge on both sides. Press it firmly against the size with your fingers. This will loosen the tissue backing, which should now be removed. Pick up another strip of leaf by the tissue, lay it lengthways on the same edge, overlapping one end of the first strip by at least 3 mm (photograph 2). Continue laying overlapping strips of leaf around the edge of the box.

Do not worry about wrinkles. When the edge is entirely covered, hit the surface of the gold lightly with the edge of your hand along its length (see photograph 3). Do this all the way around the box to smooth and flatten the leaf into the size. Next, dab leaf lightly but briskly with a 5 cm wad of cotton wool to polish the surface and remove excess leaf. Wait 24 hours, then varnish the leaf to prevent tarnishing. When the varnish dries, fill the box (see "Framing", page 30) and replace the glass cover.

4: Carefully coat the area you want to gild with quick size, placing the chair on its back on a box or table while you work.

5: With the top cover of the book of gold leaf folded back and under the book, hold the tissue away from the leaf and sweep the book gently over the sized surface so the free edge of leaf touches the size. As your hand continues its sweep, the leaf will be pulled from the book and will adhere to the sized surface.

6: Polish the leaf with cotton wool after the sized area is totally covered. The leaf is so fragile that the excess will crumble away.

Furniture and Finishes
Gold Leafing a Carved Chair

Gold leaf can be used to enhance the carving on wooden furniture, as in the chair shown on page 65. The procedure for gilding the chair can be used to gold-leaf almost any surface that is hard, smooth and non-porous and does not have complex carving. This technique requires relatively flat, accessible areas, such as those on the chair back. It is not satisfactory for use on deep, complex carvings which are filled with fine detail.

Before starting, make sure the surface you are gilding is sound. If you are re-finishing the chair, complete this, and then wait a week to let the finish dry.

In addition to the piece of furniture to be gilded you will need steel wool; 115 g of quick gold size; yellow pigment; a roll of absorbent cotton wool; flat and round camel-brushes of the right size for the work (see page 66); solvents suitable for the size and varnish (check container labels); two books of glass-grade gold leaf; and polyurethane varnish.

Preparing the surface
Rub the area you are gilding with steel wool, or use a paint scraper and fine sandpaper, and wipe away any dust with a large piece of cotton wool moistened with solvent. Mix 115 g of quick gold size with one tablespoon of yellow pigment and coat the areas you will gild with a camel-hair brush. Paint only the areas to be gold-leafed (photograph 4).

Applying loose gold leaf
When the size on the chair is dry but tacky—use the "knuckle test" (page 67)—start applying leaf to the surface. Loose gold leaf is so fragile that even a brisk puff of air can disintegrate it. Do not try to lift it with your fingers. Pick up the whole book instead and fold the cover back so it creases about 1.5 cm from the spine. Press it back under the bottom cover.

Holding the book at the spine between your thumb and forefinger, fold the tissue covering the first leaf of gold back and under, just as you did the cover of the book. Next, sweep the whole book gently over the sized area of the chair so that the free edge of the exposed leaf touches the size. This edge will stick to the first section by at least 3 mm. Continue applying and overlapping leaf in into place. Fold back the next tissue and repeat this procedure, overlapping the first section by at least 3 mm. Continue applying and overlapping leaf in this manner until the sized surface is covered with gold leaf.

Now, using a clean, flat camel-hair brush, pat the leaf into any corners in the carving. Tap the gold very lightly with the flat side of the tip of the brush. Do not use a brushing motion.

Correcting flaws
Polish the gold-leafed surface by pressing it lightly with a pad of cotton wool (photograph 6) to burnish the gold and remove excess leaf. Some gilders discard flakes of excess gold. Others save them in a clean, tightly capped jar for patching small imperfections. To do this, just breathe on the tip of a small, round camel-hair brush, pick up a flake and place it on the spot to be covered.

Another way of correcting flaws is to hold the book as you did to cover the size originally and pat the entire gilded area with the exposed leaf. Wherever a bare spot of size shows through the gold, a bit of leaf will tear off and cover it. When surface is fully covered, polish it again with a fresh piece of cotton wool.

Finishing touches
Chair backs are subject to abrasion that will wear away the gold over the years. Giving the leaf a coat of polyurethane varnish will protect the finish and is a good idea, even though the varnish will dull the lustre of the gold slightly. On the other hand the gold leaf does not tarnish or discolour, so if the article is one that is touched infrequently, such as a picture frame or mirror, this step is unnecessary.

This dish was embellished with bands of gold leaf held to the underside with water size. The texture of the centre band was created by stippling a layer of varnish before gilding.

Glass and Plastics
Gold on Glassware

If you want to gild a dish like the one above, choose one of clear glass with a smooth, even underside where the gold will be applied. The one I selected is 20 cm in diameter. The centre disc is 10 cm in diameter with a fish design etched in the bottom. The outer band is 5 cm wide.

The gold leaf, applied to the bottom of the dish, shows through the glass when the dish is placed right side up. The design was achieved by gilding a 1.3 cm stripe of plain gold around the rim, another stripe—6 mm wide—around the centre disc, and gilding the area between them with stippled gold.

To gild a dish like this one, you will need one book of glass gold; two gelatine capsules; a gilding tip (see page 70 and photographs 9 to 12); flat camel-hair brushes; a 5 to 7.5 cm wide, good quality household paint brush for applying size; half a litre of rubbing varnish (if you cannot find rubbing varnish, use a slow-drying synthetic varnish); cottonwool; glass cleaner; a fine felt-tipped pen; a 4 litre paint tin; and 1 tablespoon of Japan black (a finish sign painters mix with varnish and use to back up gold leaf; you can substitute black enamel for the Japan black/varnish mix.) You also need 55 g of damar varnish used for the stippling on the plate that is later gilded.

About two weeks before you gild the dish, open the damar varnish and leave it uncapped until it has the consistency of honey. Now you can begin. Wash the dish with detergent and water and dry it. Using the felt pen, draw two circles on the front of the dish around the band to be stippled, thus marking the edges of the inner and outer stripes of plain gold. The outer circle should be 1.3 cm in from the rim and the inner circle should be 6 mm away from the centre disc (Figure A). Draw these circles by holding the dish face-up in one hand and bracing one finger of the pen hand against the rim of the dish. Holding the pen steady, rotate the dish with the fingers of the other hand. This provides an accurate circle.

Place the dish upside down on the paint tin. From this point on, avoid touching the bottom of the dish with your fingers since any oil or grease on the

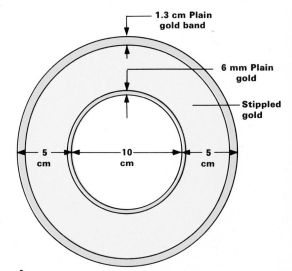

A

Figure A: The inner and outer stripes on the band of the dish are gilded with plain gold, the space between them stippled. The dish's central disc is not gilded.

69

surface will prevent the leaf from adhering to the glass. When you move the dish, slide your fingers beneath the rim and lift the dish, slipping your hand underneath it so it rests upside down on your hand. Reverse this procedure to put the dish back on the tin.

With the dish in position, scrub it with cottonwool dipped in glass cleaner and wipe off any residue. If you need to steady the dish while doing this, hold it down with your fingers on the centre disc, where you will not apply any leaf.

Next prepare water size that will hold the gold to the glass. Heat one cup of water until it comes to a boil. Reduce the heat until the boiling stops, and while the water is still hot, drop one gelatine capsule into it and stir until the capsule is completely dissolved. With a 5 to 7.5 cm wide household paint brush, cover the inner and outer bands of the dish with size.

7: With the cover of the gold-leaf book folded back and creased, press back the top tissue. Use a sheet of cardboard as a palette for the book.

8: Cut the gold leaf lightly with your fingernail, or use a fairly sharp, grease-free knife. If it wrinkles, blow on it very gently to straighten it.

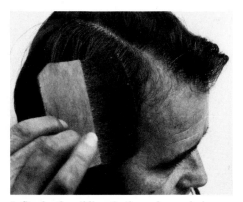

9: Stroke the gilding tip through your hair several times. This will make the gold leaf stick to the brush so you can pick it up.

10: Touch the gilding tip to the leaf and pull. The gold will snap away from the book at the cut you have made.

11: Holding the leaf almost parallel to the surface, touch it to the dish at its free edge. The water size will pull it from the brush.

Using a gilding tip

After sizing the bands of the dish, use a gilding tip to pick up a gold leaf from the book and transfer it to the band. Begin by placing the book of leaf on a 12.5 cm square of heavy cardboard. Fold back the top cover of the book to within about 2.5 cm of the spine of the book. Bend back the tissue covering the first sheet of gold (photograph 7), and cut the leaf by running your fingernail, or a sharp knife, lightly across it next to the crease in the tissue.

Brush the gilding tip through your hair a few times (photograph 9); this will make the leaf stick to the brush. Some gilders say that the static electricity thus generated holds the leaf to the brush; others claim that the oil in your hair makes the brush slightly sticky. All agree the method works.

Touch the side of the brush to the exposed leaf of gold (photograph 10) and pull it, removing the leaf from the book. Touch the end of the leaf to the prepared surface (photograph 11); the wet size will pull the leaf from the gilding tip as you withdraw it. Do not allow the brush itself to touch the size.

Keep laying leaves of gold on the bands of the dish, overlapping all edges by at least 3 mm, until both the inner and outer stripes are completely covered and overlapped. Wait for about an hour for the size to dry, at which point the gold will have become bright. Press the surface with a 5 cm pad of cottonwool to remove any gold that is not held in place by size. Inspect the surface for cracks or holes. If you find one or two, re-size the flawed areas—working very lightly to avoid softening the size already beneath the gold. Then apply leaf over the flaws with the gilding tip. If there are many flaws, you may find it is easier to apply another complete layer of leaf over the entire area.

Again, wait for the size to dry and polish the surface with cottonwool. Then rinse the size brush in warm water and use it to wash gilt surface with hot water and a light touch. This will increase the brightness of the gold, help to conceal the joints between pieces of leaf and prevent cloudiness in the size. When the surface is dry, give it a final polishing with cotton wool.

Backing up the gold

When you look at the bottom of the plate at this stage, you will see a general gilded area, but no sharply defined inner and outer stripes. These you can create by "backing up the gold"—painting stripes directly over the gold leaf with a mixture of varnish and Japan black, then scrubbing the surface after the paint dries to remove excess gold. The gold leaf that is not backed up by paint will be scrubbed away, the gold under the paint will remain in place. When the dish is right side up, you see two crisp gold stripes.

Start by mixing 1 tablespoon of Japan black with 115 g of rubbing varnish. Using flat camel-hair brushes, paint the inner and outer stripes (photograph 12) with the mixture. The circles originally drawn on the front of the dish will show faintly through the gold and serve as guide lines. Let the varnish dry for at least 24 hours; then scrub away the excess gold with glass cleaner on a cottonwool wad. Use additional wads to remove the glass cleaner.

Creating a stippled effect

When the back of the dish is dry, brush the thickened damar varnish into the area between the inner and outer stripes. Wait until the varnish becomes firm —this will take about 20 minutes to an hour. Test it by drawing a design with a dull point, such as the end of a brush handle. If the varnish returns to a smooth surface, wait and try again. If it holds the design, stipple the whole area between the bands with any desired pattern.

Put the dish aside for a week to allow the varnish to dry thoroughly. Once the varnish is set, mix a fresh batch of water size and gild the stippled area exactly as you did the inner and outer bands. Finally, give the whole gilded area a coat of rubbing varnish, overlapping the ungilded glass slightly at the outer and inner edges. When the final coat of varnish is dry, the dish is complete. It can be washed by hand with mild detergent and lukewarm water. Do not put it in a dishwasher or let it soak in a basin.

12: Use your free arm as a brace to support your brush hand while you paint a mixture of Japan black and varnish over the gold that is to remain in the inner and outer stripes. When the mixture is dry, rub the back of the dish with glass cleaner. The unprotected gold not backed up by paint will be scrubbed away.

Graphic Arts
Lettering a Sign in Gold

To gild a sign you will need one book of patent gold leaf; 115 g of clear, glossy polyurethane varnish; 115 g of quick gold size; yellow pigment; round and flat camel-hair brushes; a prepared signboard or a piece of 2.5 mm clear white pine; coarse and fine sandpaper; a fretsaw or jigsaw; heavy paper; a pounce wheel (a toothed wheel for perforating patterns, such as is used in sewing); a 46 cm square of closely woven fabric (a worn-out dress shirt would be a good source); talcum powder; drawing pins; stiff paper or cardboard; and pattern paper (brown wrapping paper will do).

For lettering your sign, you can use the alphabet in Figure B on the next page. If you want a type style you feel is better suited to the sign you have in mind, art supply shops stock alphabets in many styles and sizes.

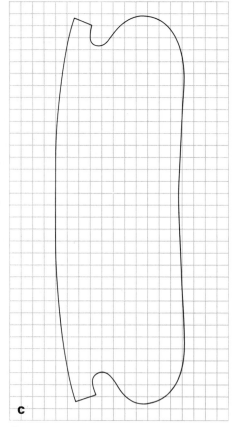

Figure C: This signboard pattern can be enlarged to any size. Measure the longest edge of the board you need for your sign in centimetres and divide by 33. This figure will be the gauge, or width in centimetres of the grid square, needed to enlarge the pattern.

ABCDEFGHIJK
LMNOPQRSTU
VWXYZ&

B

Figure B: Enlarge the letters to be used in your sign to whatever size you like, draw them on heavy paper or cardboard and cut them out, according to instructions below and on page 49.

Making a pattern

Measure the height you want your lettering to be (bearing in mind the proportionate length) and divide this figure by eight to give you the pattern gauge. Trace each letter you will need for your sign or enlarge it on a piece of stiff paper or cardboard, using the method described on page 49. Cut the letters out of the heavy paper or cardboard, making one copy of each letter for every time it appears in the sign.

Use a ruler to draw a straight line on the pattern paper and, aligning the cut-out letters on the line, arrange them just as you want them to appear on the finished sign. Tack the letters into place with two or three drawing pins each. Then trace each letter on the pattern paper and remove the cut-outs.

Now sketch the shape of the sign on the pattern paper. The lettering should fill the space comfortably without looking crowded. If you select a simple rectangle for the sign, measure the width and depth of the outline sketched on the pattern and order a prepared signboard from a sign company. If you prefer starting from scratch, cut the sign from a length of 25 mm clear white pine.

Cutting and finishing a signboard

If you wish to make a signboard like the one shown in Figure C, decide the width of the sign in centimetres and divide this figure by 33. The result will be the gauge to enlarge the pattern according to instructions on page 49.

Cut out the signboard pattern, trace it on the piece of white pine, and cut the shape out with a fretsaw or jigsaw. (I moulded the edge of the sign I made with a plane, but you can round the edges with sandpaper.)

Sand the signboard to a smooth surface, using coarse and then smooth sandpaper. Wipe away dust with a rag moistened with turpentine or paint thinner. The sign can now be stained; I chose dark walnut. Follow the stain with three coats of clear, glossy polyurethane varnish, allowing 24 hours between coats. Rub the finish lightly with steel wool between coats and wipe it free of dust with a rag moistened with thinner.

Put the sign aside for a week to let the varnish dry completely. Different varnishes have different drying times, and although most varnishes feel dry to the touch and can be smoothed and re-coated in less than 24 hours, some remain faintly tacky much longer.

Transferring the pattern

While the signboard is drying, the pounce bag can be made. Pour about a cup of talcum powder on to the centre of a 46 cm square of closely woven fabric, placing a handful of absorbent cottonwool on top of the talc and gathering up the edges of the fabric to form a bag. Close the neck of the bag with five or six turns of masking tape.

Next, spread a thick towel or blanket on your work table and place the letter pattern over it. Hold the pattern steady with one hand and with the other, roll the toothed edge of the pounce wheel over the outlines of the letters. When you have finished, hold the pattern up to the light to make sure that all the lines have been perforated. Put the pattern down and retrace any lines that you may have missed.

When the varnished signboard has dried thoroughly, centre the perforated pattern on it and tack it in place with drawing pins. Now tap the pounce bag on the pattern wherever there are tracings for the lettering (photograph 13). The talcum powder in the bag will fall through the perforations in the pattern and form the letter outlines on the sign in a series of white dots. Make sure the letters have been completely transferred by lifting a corner of the pattern, then remove the drawing pins and pattern carefully so the pattern does not slide against the talcum dots and smear them.

Painting the letters

The next step is to paint the letters on the sign with quick gold size. Position the signboard on your work table and run a length of masking tape along the bottom of the lettering, outlined on the board so that the top of the strip of tape forms the bottom edge of each letter. Do the same at the top of the letters. These two strips of tape will keep tops and bottoms of the letters aligned.

Mix 115 g of quick gold size with 1 tablespoon of yellow pigment and paint in the letters using a flat camel-hair brush slightly narrower than the width of the lines you are painting. A round brush can be used later to fill in corners and other areas with fine detail.

Steady your hand with a mahlstick as you paint (photograph 14). You can buy one in a paint shop or make one by nailing a large cork to one end of a dowel 60 cm long and 2.5 cm in diameter. When you paint, hold the mahlstick in your free hand, resting the cork against your work table. Brace your brush hand against the stick to steady it as you paint.

Painting the letters neatly is the most difficult part of making a sign, and it helps to practice beforehand. Pounce the design on a sheet of blank paper, tack it down and paint in the letters, using paint left over from some other job. Do this several times until you feel you can paint the sign easily.

When you do paint the sign, work at a comfortable pace. Do not rush, but do avoid going so slowly that your hand shakes or hesitates and produces a ragged line. Do not worry about mistakes: If your hand slips, clean the area with some cottonwool moistened with thinner and paint it again.

Applying the leaf

When all the letters are covered with size, wait about 20 minutes, then use your knuckle to test the tackiness of the last letter you painted. When the size is ready (see page 67), begin applying patent gold to the letters.

Pick up a leaf of patent gold by the tissue and lay it over the first sized letter of the sign. Cover the letter completely, but do not let the leaf touch the next letter. This will prevent seams from appearing within the letters. Peel the tissue from the gold. Pick up a second leaf of gold in the same way and apply it to the second letter, taking care not to let it touch the third letter. If it overlaps the first letter that is already gilded, it does not matter. Continue in this manner until every letter is covered with a leaf of gold. Then polish the surface with a pad of cottonwool.

After the surface is polished, pick up a leaf of gold by the tissue and pat the whole gilded surface with it to cover any bare spots in the leaf. Polish the surface once again with cottonwool and let the size dry for 24 hours. Finally, give the sign a finishing coat of clear, glossy polyurethane varnish.

13: With the letter pattern tacked to the sign, pat the surface with the talc-filled pounce bag.

14: Steady your hand with a mahlstick when you paint the letters with quick gold size. Tape at top and bottom helps to keep them even.

GRANNY SQUARES
Patchwork Crochet

By Connie Kuznekoff

For everyone who likes to crochet, granny squares provide a good way to use odd pieces of yarn left over from other projects. A granny square is a crocheted shape that starts with chain stitches slip-stitched into a ring. The first round is worked into the ring, the second round into the first round; five such rounds make the traditional granny square. Each round is made of groups of treble crochet stitches separated by chain stitches. Directions for making these basic stitches are in Crochet Craftnotes, pages 84 to 85.

The traditional square was usually made with 4-ply knitting yarn, and its dimensions varied slightly according to the size of the hook used. Today's granny squares may differ in several ways from the ones our grandmothers made. They now can include any stitch or combination of stitches used in crocheting. And squares are no longer used only for afghans. They can be made into clothing such as the cap and scarf on page 80, or accessories such as the roomy tote bag on page 82. Knitting wool is still the yarn most often used, but any weight yarn, jute, or even string can be made into a granny square. The place mat on page 78 is made with string.

You can crochet granny squares in the specific colour combinations suggested in the directions for each project, or you can arrange left-over yarn to create your own designs. The number of colours used and the way they are arranged make the work interesting. Since you crochet only one square at a time, you can carry the work with you wherever you go.

Needlecrafts
Traditional Afghan

Sixty-three granny squares in two harmonious colour combinations are used in this traditional afghan (far left in the photograph opposite). The squares are simple to make because you use only the chain stitch, slip stitch, and treble crochet (see Crochet Craftnotes, pages 84 to 85). To adapt the directions to your scrap yarn, vary the colours for rounds 1 to 4, but use only one colour for round 5 on all squares.

Size: Approx. 81 by 103 cm.
Materials: Of 4-ply knitting yarn allow 114 g each of dark turquoise, peach, light blue, aqua, dark rose; 228 g each of violet and green. Crochet hook size 4.50, or size needed to obtain tension. A tapestry needle.
Tension: Each square is 11.5 by 11.5 cm.
Main square: With dark turquoise, ch 5 and join with a sl st to form ring. *Rnd. 1*: Ch 3, 2 tr in ring, *ch 1, 3 tr in ring; repeat from * twice more, ch 1, and join with sl st to top of ch 3 at beginning. Fasten off. *Rnd. 2*: Join peach in any ch 1 space, ch 3, 2 tr in same sp, *ch 1, then 3 tr, ch 1, 3 tr all in next sp; repeat from * twice more, ch 1, 3 tr in same sp as first ch 3, ch 1, join. Fasten off. *Rnd 3*: Join violet in any ch 1 corner sp, ch 3, 2 tr in same sp, *ch 1, 3 tr in next sp, ch 1, in corner sp work (3 tr, ch 1, 3 tr); repeat from * twice more, ch 1, 3 tr in

The three afghans opposite show the diversity possible with granny squares. The traditional granny-square afghan (far left) has a muted, harmonious colour scheme. The afghan in shades of blue (centre left) uses a pattern with a floral centre. The bright red-and-white afghan (near left) is made with a raised stitch called the popcorn stitch.

The look of the traditional granny square changes with different colour emphasis. The contrasting squares above are used as a border on two sides, and the outer edge is a row of treble crochet.

next sp, ch 1, 3 tr in same sp as first ch 3, ch 1, join. Fasten off. *Rnd 4*: Join light blue, and work as rnd 3, but working 1 extra group of 3 tr and 1 ch between corners. Fasten off. *Rnd 5*: Join green and work as rnd 3, but working 2 extra groups of 3 tr and 1 ch between corners. Fasten off.

Contrasting square: Follow directions for main square using peach for ring and rnd 1, aqua for rnd 2, violet for rnd 3, rose for rnd 4, and green for rnd 5. Make 14 squares.

Joining: Join main squares together 7 squares across and 7 squares down. Join contrasting squares into 2 strips of 7 squares each; sew strips each end of afghan. See Craftnotes below and opposite for details on joining and blocking.

Border: Join dark turquoise in any tr and ch 3, * 1 tr in each st and 1 tr in each seam to corner, 3 tr into corner sp; repeat from * 3 times, work 1 tr in each st to ch 3 at beginning, join. Fasten off.

CRAFTNOTES: BLOCKING

The blocking of articles made of granny squares—the process whereby the squares are squared up—can be done in one of two ways. The granny squares can be blocked individually, but this is extremely time-consuming and should be done only if a square seems very distorted. To prepare such a square for blocking, pin it wrong side up to a flat surface—measuring to make sure that the dimensions of the square are the same as those given in the directions— and proceed as described on the right for blocking assembled articles.

For most granny-square projects, blocking can be done after the squares are joined and borders completed. This is the quick way. Pin the assembled unit securely to an ironing board or work table, measuring so the article is same size as dimensions given in directions.

With an iron set on "wool" and using a dampened pressing cloth, lightly pass the iron over the granny squares. Do not rest the full weight of the iron on the article. Let the work become completely dry before unpinning it.

CRAFTNOTES: JOINING SQUARES

To complete any granny square project, individual squares must be joined. First, all yarn ends should be woven into the back of each square and trimmed. With experience, you will find it easy to conceal yarn ends on one round when crocheting the next round. This requires placing the yarn end along the stitch into which you are crocheting, so that the stitch you are working will conceal both the top of the stitch on the previous row and the yarn end. (See "Fastening Yarn" in Crochet Craftnotes, page 85).

Squares may be sewn or crocheted together. Sewing provides a flat finish and works better when you are easing or fitting a larger square to a smaller one. Always work on the wrong side of the squares and use matching yarn (contrasting yarn is shown in the photographs only for clarity). The best way to assemble a number of squares for an afghan is to sew them together into strips of the desired length and then join the strips to the width you want. Sewing strips is easier than sewing squares because you do not have to knot and cut the yarn so often, and strips keep the granny squares better organized. When joining multicolour squares, arrange them on a table until you have achieved a pleasing effect, then join them as they are positioned.

After threading a tapestry needle with a 45 cm length of yarn and tying a slip knot in one end, slip needle through the bottom two loops of corner chain (left above). Insert needle into bottom two loops of second square (right) and through the slip knot, pulling to tighten knot.

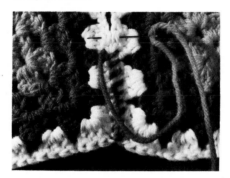

Working from the lower edge towards upper edge and right to left, insert needle through bottom two loops of last round in right square and the adjacent two loops of the last round in left square. Sew in this manner, matching squares stitch for stitch and concealing any yarn end in with stitches.

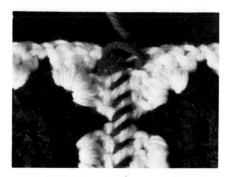

To fasten yarn at upper edge, take two stitches at corner chains, and before pulling second stitch tight, insert needle through stitch as shown above. Finish by pulling tight and weaving a short length of yarn into square before cutting.

When sewing strips together, use a cross stitch formed by stitching a second stitch over first one, as shown, to reinforce corners so they will match more evenly. Except at the corners, use the same procedure for sewing strips as you do for sewing squares together.

To crochet squares together, place them with right sides together, attach yarn to the top loop of each corner, then slip stitch for the length of squares as shown. To finish, fasten off at end of squares and weave yarn end in on the back.

Needlecrafts
Place Mat

Ordinary fine household string was used to make the durable 30 by 38 cm place mat shown below. The centre is a traditional granny square enlarged to 10 rows. To make the square into a rectangle, 3 rows of treble crochet were added to the opposite sides.

Size: 30 by 38 cm.

Materials: Approx. 155 m of fine string for each place mat. Crochet hook size 5.00 or size needed to obtain tension.

Tension: Square is 25 by 25 cm. 4 stitches to 2.5 cm over the treble crochet sides.

Square: Follow directions for granny square (page 75) but make 10 rows. The last row has eight groups of 3 tr plus the corners for each side.

Side: *Row 1*: Join the string to one corner, ch 3, 1 tr in each tr and 1 tr in each sp to end, ch 3, turn. *Row 2*: 1 tr in each tr to end, ch 3, turn. *Row 3*: Repeat row 2. Fasten off. Join string to one corner of opposite of square and repeat the rows 1 to 3 as for first side. Do not fasten off at end of last row but work all round outer edge of mat for border, working 1 tr in each tr and 3 tr in each corner to end, join. Fasten off.

This place mat is one large granny square with three rows of treble crochet added to two opposite sides to make a rectangle. The natural colour of the string is attractive in this setting.

Light blue floral centres stand out against the darker blue background colours of the square in this afghan. The scalloped border adds an unusual finishing touch.

Needlecrafts
Floral Granny-square Afghan

Although 180 squares are required for the 107 by 134 cm afghan (above and centre in the photograph on page 74), the 9 cm squares and the scalloped border work up quickly as you gain experience. Use scrap yarn or your three favourite colours. The design also makes a lovely baby afghan if worked in a smaller size such as 9 squares by 15 squares.

Size: 107 by 134 cm.

Materials: Of 4-ply knitting yarn allow 341 g of light blue; 454 g of medium blue; 567 g of dark blue. Crochet hook size 4.50 or size needed to obtain tension; a tapestry needle.

Tension: Each square is 9 by 9 cm.

Squares: With light blue, ch 4, join with a sl st to form ring. *Rnd 1*: *1 dc in ring, ch 10; repeat from * 7 times, join with sl st to first dc and fasten off. *Rnd 2*: With medium blue, join yarn in any ch 10 loop, ch 3, 2 tr in same space, * in next loop work 3 tr, ch 2, 3 tr, for corner, 3 tr in next loop; repeat from * twice more, 3 tr, ch 2, 3 tr all in next loop for corner, join. Fasten off. *Rnd 3*: With dark blue, join yarn in any ch 2 corner sp, ch 3, 2 tr in same sp, * 1 tr in each tr to next corner sp, 3 tr in corner sp; repeat from * twice more, 1 tr in each

tr of last side, join and fasten off. Make 180 squares.

Joining: Sew squares together to make afghan 12 squares wide and 15 squares long. See Craftnotes on page 77 for details.

Border: With medium blue, join yarn in centre tr of any corner and ch 1, 2 dc in same st, 1 dc in each tr of squares and 1 dc in each seam between squares, continue in this way working 3 dc in each corner tr all round afghan, join and fasten off. With light blue, join yarn in any centre dc at corner, * sl st in next dc, 1 dc in next dc, 1 tr in next dc, 3 tr in next dc, 1 tr in next dc, 1 dc in next dc; repeat from * all round afghan working 2 or 3 sl sts at corners to keep design even. Join with a sl st to beginning and fasten off. This border is distinctive yet simple to do.

Cap and scarf were co-ordinated with the navy coat by working the last row of each square and the scalloped border on the scarf in navy. Inner rows of the squares use six bright colours in various combinations.

Needlecrafts
Cap-and-scarf Set

The squares used to make the bright cap and scarf pictured (left) are the same kind of squares as those used in the floral afghan (page 79), but each square has an additional row of treble crochet stitches to make it larger. The cap is made with four of these 13 cm squares sewn together with one smaller 10 cm square for the crown. The scarf is made with 24 of the larger squares.

Size: Cap fits head sizes 51 to 64 cm. For sizes 41 to 51 cm use 10 cm squares. Scarf about 30 by 158 cm.

Materials: Of double knitting yarn allow 142 g each of light blue, pink, rose, lime, green and purple; 284 g of navy. Crochet hook size 4.50 or size needed for tension; a tapestry needle.

Tension: Large square is 13 by 13 cm. Small square is 10 by 10 cm.

Large square: Follow crochet directions for floral afghan square on page 79 for rnds 1 and 2. *Rnd 3*: With desired colour, join yarn in any ch-2 corner sp, ch 3, 2 tr in same sp, * (3 tr in next sp between 3 tr groups) twice, work (3 tr, ch 2, 3 tr) in next ch-2 sp

at corner; repeat from * twice, 3 tr in each of next 2 sp, 3 tr, ch 2, join with sl st to ch 3 at beginning. Fasten off.

Rnd 4: Work as rnd 3 of floral afghan square. When making large squares, alternate colours as desired for rnds 1, 2 and 3. Use navy for rnd 4. Make 28 squares: 24 for the scarf and 4 for the cap.

Small square: Follow the directions for floral afghan square; use desired colours for rnds 1 and 2, navy for rnd 3.

Blocking: For cap, block squares before joining. Scarf is blocked after it is completed. See Craftnotes on page 76.

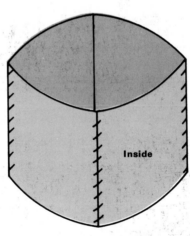

A

Figure A: To make the body of the cap, join the sides of four large granny squares so they form a circle. Seams should be on the inside so they will not show when the cap is completed.

B

Figure B: To make the crown, sew a small square to one end of circle, fitting large squares to the small one so the corners of small squares match seams between the larger squares.

Joining cap: For larger cap size, join 4 large squares together in a circle (Figure A). Sew small square to top of cap, easing the large squares to the smaller one matching the corners of small square to seams of larger ones (Figure B). For smaller cap size, join 4 small squares together in a circle (Figure A) and sew another small square on top for the crown, matching corners.

Border: Join navy to any tr along edge of cap, ch 1, 1 dc in each tr and each seam round edge, join with a sl st to first dc. *Next rnd*: Work 1 dc in each dc round cap, join. Repeat the last rnd once more. Fasten off.

Joining scarf: Sew squares together 12 squares long and 2 squares wide in alternating colours.

Border: Follow directions for floral afghan using navy for both rows.

A granny-square afghan can look modern rather than old-fashioned. The bold geometric look of this design is due to the use of only two colours, with their sequence reversed in the border squares.

Needlecrafts
Popcorn granny-square Afghan

The circles within the squares of this afghan (above and far right in the photograph on page 74) use a raised design called the popcorn stitch for a textured effect. The popcorn stitch, made of 5 treble crochet stitches (Figure C), is easy to master. I chose to use only two colours for the afghan, with the colour sequence reversed in the squares used as a border.

Size: Approx. 86 by 96 cm.
Tension: Square is 10 by 10 cm.
Materials: Of 4-ply knitting yarn allow 567 g each of red and white. Crochet hook size 4.50 or size needed to obtain tension. A tapestry needle.

Main square: With white, ch 4, join with a sl st to form ring. *Rnd 1*: Ch 3, 15 tr in ring, join with sl st to ch 3 (16 tr). *Rnd 2*: Ch 4, *1 tr in next tr, ch 1; repeat from * 14 times, join with a sl st to 3rd of 4 ch. Fasten off. *Rnd 3*: Join red in any ch-1 sp, ch 3, 4 tr in same sp, drop loop from hook, insert hook in top of ch 3, pick up loop and draw through, ch 2 (popcorn made), * 5 tr in next sp, drop loop from hook, insert hook in 1st of 5 tr, pick up loop and draw through, ch 2, repeat from * 14 times (16 popcorns), join. Fasten off. *Rnd 4*: Join white in any ch-2 sp, ch 3, 2 tr in same sp, *(3 tr in next ch-2 sp) 3 times, in next sp work (3 tr, ch 2, 3 tr) for corner, repeat from * twice, 3 tr in each ch-2 sp of last side, 3 tr in corner, ch 2, join. Fasten off. *Rnd 5*: Join red in

and ch 2 corner sp, ch 1, 2 dc in same sp, work 1 dc in each tr and 3 dc in each corner sp to end of round, join. Fasten off. Make 42 squares.

Contrasting square: Follow instructions for main square, reversing colour sequence and working the ring and rnds 1, 2 and 4 in red, rnds 3 and 5 in white. Make 30 squares.

Joining: Join main squares together 6 squares across and 7 squares down. Join contrasting squares so there are 2 strips of 6 squares and 2 strips of 9 squares. Sew the shorter contrasting strips across the ends and longer strips down sides of afghan (Figure D).

Border: With red, join yarn to centre dc of any corner, ch 3, 1 tr in same dc, work 1 tr in each dc and seam, and 2 tr in each centre dc at corners to end of rnd, join. *Next rnd*: Ch 4, 1 tr in same place as ch 4, * ch 1, miss 1 tr, 1 tr in next tr; repeat from * to next corner, work (1 tr, ch 1, 1 tr) all in corner tr. Continue in this way all round afghan, join. Fasten off.

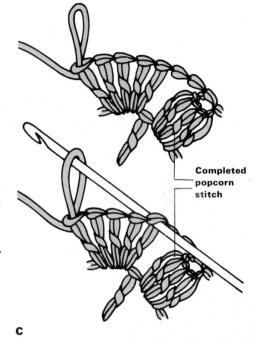

C

Figure C: To make a popcorn, work five treble crochet stitches in the space between treble crochet stitches in the previous row, and drop the loop (top). Insert hook in top of first treble crochet, pick up the loop (bottom), and pull through. The stitch on the right of stitch being worked is a completed popcorn stitch.

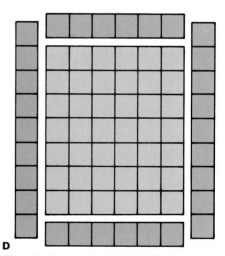

D

Figure D: Join main squares of the popcorn afghan so the body is 6 squares by 7 squares. Then join contrasting squares into two strips of 6 squares (for the top and bottom) and two strips of 9 squares (for the sides).

The combination of geometric shapes and a bold colour scheme gives a look of contemporary fashion to this commodious carryall.

Needlecrafts
Shoulder Tote Bag

Earthy tones of brown, gold and orange were used for the soft-sided shoulder tote bag shown in the photograph on the left. Its 38 by 38 by 6 cm dimensions give it a generous capacity. Each side is made of nine 13 cm squares; the band joining the sides and handle is made of a continuous strip of treble crochet.

Size: 38 by 38 by 6 cm deep. Handle portion is 88 cm long.

Materials: Of 4-ply knitting yarn allow 113 g each of orange, beige, gold, and rust; 227 g of dark brown. Crochet hook size 4.50; a tapestry needle; 1.55 m of 5 cm wide petersham ribbon; 1 m of 2.5 cm petersham ribbon; a piece of heavy-weight material for lining.

Tension: Squares are 13 by 13 cm. Handle tension is 4 treble to 2.5 cm.

Squares: Follow directions for popcorn afghan squares, alternating colours for rnds 1, 2, 3 and 4. Use dark brown rnd 5 only. Make 18 squares.

Joining: Join squares for sides, 3 squares by 3 squares. Alternate squares to vary colours. From right side using dark brown work in dc along top edge of bag. Fasten off. Block sides of tote after squares have

been joined as described on page 76.

The handle and band: Join dark brown yarn at lower edge in centre of middle square, ch 1, then work 1 dc in each st and each seam to corner, work in the same way up side edge of bag to top, now make 134 ch for handle, join ch to other side of top edge, work in dc down side of bag and then along lower edge to first dc worked, join.
Next rnd: Ch 3, work 1 tr in each dc and each ch all round bag and handle, join. Repeat the last rnd 3 times more. Then work 1 rnd of dc in each tr. Fasten off.

The under handle: With dark brown: make 140 ch. *1st Row*: 1 tr in 4th ch from hook, 1 tr in each ch to end, turn. *2nd Row*: Ch 3, 1 tr in each tr to end, turn. Repeat the last row twice more. *Next Row*: Ch 1, 1 dc in each tr to end. Fasten off.

Assembling tote: Each side of the tote bag is made of nine squares sewn together to make a larger square. The 5 cm wide band between the sides and the 5 cm wide handle is one continuous strip of double crochet that is crocheted directly on to one of the granny-square sides (see directions for the handle and band above). To join the other side, work on inside of the tote and

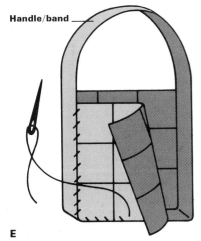

Handle/band

E

Figure E: Crochet the handle and band, one continuous strip, to one of the granny-square sides. Working from the inside, sew the second side to the band along three sides, using yarn and a tapestry needle.

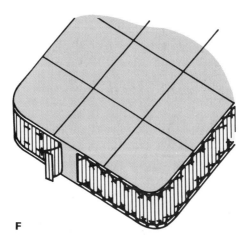

F

Figure F: Sew a 5.5 cm wide ribbon reinforcement all around the inside of the treble crochet handle and band, using small stitches. Lap the ends where they meet.

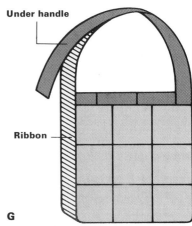

Under handle

Ribbon

G

Figure G: With the bag turned inside out, place the crocheted under handle over the ribbon reinforcement on the handle (as shown) but not along the band between the granny-square sides.

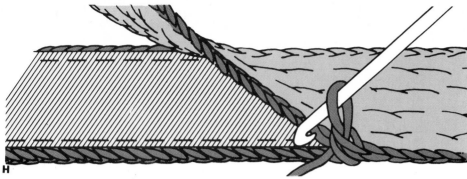

H

Figure H: With the bag right side out, attach the three layers of the handle—the handle, the ribbon reinforcement, and the under handle—with a row of double crochet on each edge of the crocheted pieces, sandwiching the ribbon between them.

sew second granny-square side to outside of the band (Figure E), along the sides and the bottom.

The band is reinforced with petersham ribbon. With the tote inside out and starting at centre bottom, pin 5 cm-wide ribbon to the inside of the entire handle and band. Lap ends and secure ribbon in place with catch stitches (Figure F). To finish the handle, the crocheted under handle (see directions on opposite page) is placed over the petersham ribbon along the handle (but not along the band between granny-square sides) (Figure G). The three layers of the handle, two layers of treble crochet with a ribbon reinforcement between them, must be crocheted together. To do this, turn tote right side out. From right side of upper handle, join dark brown yarn to top loop of upper handle above sides and top loop of 2nd stitch of the under handle. Ch 1 and work 1 row of dc through one loop of each handle section (Figure H). Fasten off at other granny-square side. Join other edge of crocheted handles in same manner, sandwiching the ribbon between handle sections.

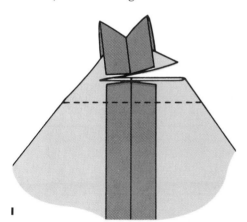

I

Figure I: Stitch seams of lining and press open, then fold corner into a triangle, stitch across the corner 2.8 cm from point of triangle, and trim corner to 1.3 cm.

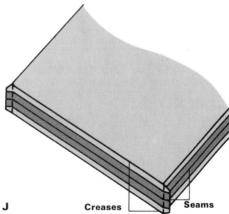

J   Creases   Seams

Figure J: Press a crease along either side of the seams of the lining from one end of the corner stitching to the other. This will make the lining fit the shape of the crocheted tote.

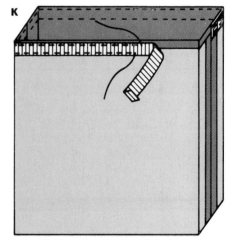

K

Figure K: Turn the top edge of the lining under 1.3 cm and press, then stitch 2.5 cm wide ribbon along the top as a reinforcement before you stitch the lining into the bag.

Lining: Cut two pieces of lining each 47.5 cm wide by 44.5 cm long. Seams of 1.3 cm are allowed. With right sides together, machine-stitch along one side of lining, across bottom, and along other side. Press seams open. Fold into triangle at corner and stitch across corner 2.8 cm from end. Trim corner 1.3 cm (Figure I). Press crease along either side of lining from one end of stitching to the other (Figure J). Turn under 1.3 cm at top of lining and press. Stitch 2.5 cm wide ribbon just inside pressed edge of lining (Figure K), and overlap edges of ribbon where they meet. Insert lining into bag, aligning side seam of lining with centre of bands and hand-sew in place just below edge along sides. Secure lining to lower edge of tote at corners with small stitches.

CROCHET

Abbreviations

ch	chain		repeat from
dec	decrease	rnd	round
dc	double crochet	sl st	slip stitch
dtc	double treble crochet	st(s)	stitch(es)
h tr	half treble crochet	tr	treble crochet
inc	increase	yo	yarn over

To increase with Afghan Stitch: At the beginning of a row, pull up a loop in the 2nd vertical bar; then insert hook under stitch between vertical bar just worked and next one. One extra loop has been added. At end of row make the increase loop between 2nd and 3rd vertical bars from the end.

To Decrease with Afghan Stitch: At the beginning of a row, slip hook under 2nd and 3rd upright bars, and draw up one loop. At the end of row, decrease in same manner on 2nd and 3rd bars from end.

To Cast Off: Work a double crochet in each stitch.

Double crochet

On a foundation chain, insert the hook into the second chain from the hook.

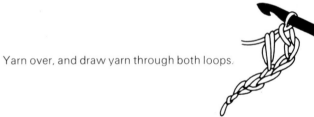

Yarn over, and draw through stitch (2 loops on hook).

Yarn over, and draw yarn through both loops.

Chain stitch

Make a slipknot, and slide on a crochet hook.

Hold crochet hook with right index finger and thumb (left if you are left-handed). Wrap yarn through fingers of other hand to provide tension, and guide with index finger.
Bring yarn over and around crochet hook.

Catch yarn on hook, and pull through existing loop. Original loop slips off. Repeat for a foundation chain.

Half treble crochet

Yarn over, and insert hook into third chain from hook.

Pull up a loop (3 loops on hook).

Yarn over, and draw through all 3 loops.

Slip stitch

Working on a foundation chain, miss one stitch, and insert hook in top strand of the second chain. Yarn over, and draw through both loops on hook.

CRAFTNOTES

Treble crochet
Yarn over, and insert hook in fourth chain from hook.

Draw up loop (3 loops on hook). Yarn over; pull through 2 loops.

Two loops remaining on hook.

Yarn over, and pull through last 2 loops.

Double treble crochet
Yarn over twice; insert hook in fifth chain from hook.

Draw up a loop (4 loops on hook).

Yarn over; draw through 2 loops (3 loops on hook).

Yarn over; draw through 2 loops (2 loops on hook).

Yarn over; pull through last 2 loops (no loops left).

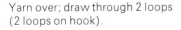

Fastening Yarn: Bring end through loop of last stitch, and cut yarn 7.5 or 10 cm long. Thread end on yarn needle, and weave along a row of stitches on the wrong side for a few centimetres. Clip excess yarn.

Blocking: On an ironing board, pin each piece of work wrong side up and to accurate measurements. Use rustproof pins. Set iron for wool, and cover work with damp cloth. Do not rest weight of iron on crocheted article, but pass iron slowly over it. Let article dry before unpinning.

Afghan stitch
Make a chain the desired length, not including loop on hook, which counts as first stitch of next row. Insert hook in second chain, and draw up a loop.

Pull up a loop in each chain, keeping all loops on hook. (This is first half of row.)

Yarn over hook, and draw through first loop.

Yarn over hook, and draw through 2 loops. Repeat with all loops on hook. (This is second half of row.)

Remaining loop is first stitch of next row.

Insert hook in second vertical bar, and draw up a loop. Proceed across row, drawing up a loop in each vertical bar and retaining them all on hook. In last stitch, insert hook through double loop, and pull up a loop.

Return as in steps 3 and 4.

HAMMOCKS AND SLINGS
Swinging Suspensions

By Joe Scheurer

A hammock is a light, portable bed that you can roll up and tuck easily under your arm, or lash to a haversack. It can be made of string, rope or canvas. Because it is suspended—between two trees, for example, or between any two points strong enough to bear the weight—what is underneath does not matter. If you are ashore, the ground may be rocky, wet or sloping; a hammock will still be comfortable. If you are aboard ship, the movement of the vessel will not dump you out of bed; the hammock will swing with the motion.

When European sailors discovered the cool string hammocks used by natives of the South Pacific and West Indies, they decided to try these beds aboard ship, and were delighted with the results. But their sea-going hammocks were made of sailcloth and rope, using techniques of stitching, splicing and knot-tying known to sailors everywhere. I designed my hammock (shown opposite) while I was a merchant seaman.

You can make a hammock like mine to roll up and take on camping trips, or just to leave hanging in your garden all summer long. But the best way to learn the techniques for making such a hammock is first to make a canvas sling that you can use to carry things. The sling shown on page 90 is a mini-version of the cargo sling used by ships at dockside to load or unload all kinds of cargo and machinery; a large sling can lift as much as half a tonne. The small one I have designed can be trusted with as many books, fireplace logs, bricks, or other heavy things as you can comfortably lift by its handles. Before you make either a sling or hammock, become familiar with the equipment you will use (described below), and learn how to make a grommet, splice rope, and do flat stitching (see Craftnotes, pages 88 and 89).

Tools and materials

To work with rope and canvas, use the sailmaker's equipment pictured in photograph 1. This may be purchased from sailmakers or marine supply shops. Tools and equipment that may be unfamiliar to you are:

Fid: A piece of smooth hardwood, pointed at one end and rounded on the other. (Use a fid to make a grommet hole if you have no hole punch, or to stretch a stitched grommet.)

Hole punch: A piece of forged steel with a round cutting edge. (Use a 1.5 cm punch to start rope holes for the hammock and sling.)

Marline: Two-ply string, sometimes called marlin, that is oiled or tarred. (Use marline to make rings that will become grommets for rope.)

Marlinspike: A pointed tool made from steel and slimmer than the fid. (Use a marlinspike to separate rope strands when making a splice.)

Palm or *sailor's sewing palm*: A device made of stiff leather and fitted like a glove, with a lead-lined cup just above the heel of the hand. (Use a palm instead of a thimble to push the needle when sewing canvas. You can buy a left-handed or right-handed sewing palm.)

Rubber: A piece of smooth hardwood for rubbing or smoothing seams and making sharp creases. (You can whittle one from an old hammer handle.)

Sail needles: Large sewing needles that are triangular near the point and cylindrical at the eye. (The wide shank of a sail needle spreads canvas weave so the twine can pass through easily; use a size 13 for the hammock and sling.)

Twine: Heavy string thicker than sewing thread but thinner than cord. (Use 10-ply waxed rayon twine or cotton tubing on hammock and sling.)

1: These sailmaker's tools and materials, reading from left to right, include: In the background, canvas and coils of 1.5 cm and 1 cm terylene or manila rope; back row, spools of rayon twine, and cotton tubing; centre row, coil of marline, clasp knife, two turns of marline coiled into a grommet ring, hammer, hole punch, hand-made seam rubber, marlinspike, small and large fids, shears; front row (next to hammer handle), sailor's palm, sail needles.

The only trick in hanging a hammock is to find two strong supports about 3 m apart. Sling the hammock from these supports so that the centre of the canvas, before anyone gets in, is 30 to 60 cm below the level of the rings on the harness (see colour photograph on page 91).

Making a stitched grommet

Canvas hammocks and slings have ropes going through them. To keep the ropes from tearing the canvas, the edges of the holes are reinforced with stitched grommets. To make a grommet, mark the location of the centre of the hole on the canvas with pencil or chalk. Place canvas on a piece of scrap hardwood. Centre a 1.5 cm diameter punch over the hole mark, and rap the punch sharply with a hammer. Hole edges should be clean-cut. If you have no punch, draw a 1.5 cm circle around the centre mark, pierce centre with a fid or an awl, and cut around the circle with a sharp knife or single-edge razor blade. Thread a No. 13 sailmaker's needle with a little more than 2 m of 10-ply waxed rayon twine, so the needle will be pulling a double strand about 1 m long.

Forming the grommet: Lay two turns of marline around a grommet hole to make a ring slightly larger than the hole, and tie marline ends with twine. Place the ring over the punched hole, and use a pencil to draw a sewing-line circle on the canvas 3 mm outside the circumference of the marline ring.

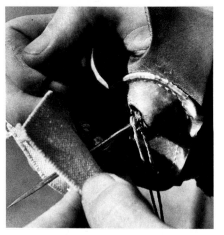

Beginning the grommet stitches: Slide a sailor's sewing palm over the top of your hand and thumb, with the strap around your palm, and begin the first stitch on the sewing line. The small lead-lined cup should be just below your thumb at the heel of your hand. Fit the eye end of the needle into this cup, and apply pressure gradually until the needle pierces the canvas. Do not move sewing palm from side to side trying to force the needle; if you do, the needle end may slip out of the cup. On the first stitch, pull all but 1.5 cm of twine through the canvas, and use the next two stitches to tie down the loose 1.5 cm of twine.

"Drawing" the radius: After each stitch, turn the canvas over and pull twine towards centre of hole, as if you were "drawing" the radius of the hole; double strands of twine should lie nearly parallel and appear to radiate from centre of hole. After "drawing" radius, pull twine outside hole and begin the next stitch on pencilled sewing line.

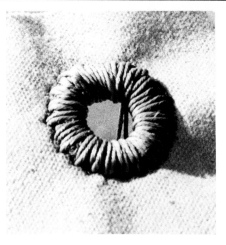

Completing the stitching: Spacing your stitches 6 mm apart, sew all the way around the grommet until the hole edges are covered with twine.

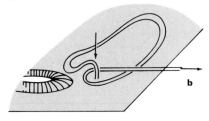

Tying off with a half hitch: With the stitching completed, tie off with a half hitch on underside of canvas. Hold loop (a) with finger and pull free end of twine (b) with other hand until the knot lies flat and tight against the canvas.

Flat stitching a canvas hem

Flat stitches for a sling or hammock hem are made with a No. 13 sailmaker's needle and waxed rayon or linen twine.

Making the crease: Fold canvas twice, so the hem is three layers thick, and use a seam rubber to make a sharp crease.

HAMMOCKS AND SLINGS

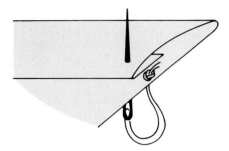

To stitch hem, pass the needle upwards through the centre of hem.

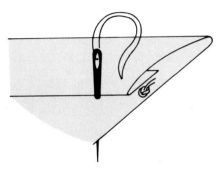

Then pass needle directly downwards on the sewing line.

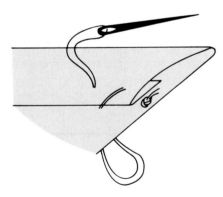

Finally, pass needle upwards through centre of hem so finished flat stitch lies on the front of the canvas at about a 60° angle to the crease. After each stitch, flatten out double strands of twine so that they lie parallel.

Permanent short splice

After you have marked the right length for a sling's handles with a square knot (see page 91), substitute a permanent short splice for the temporary square knot. Mark rope on each side of the square knot with chalk. Untie the square knot and cut off rope ends 7.5 cm above your marks. Note that each end of the rope has three strands, wound in a spiral; the direction or twist of this spiral is called

the lay of the rope. As you splice, you will weave "uphill" or against the lay or spiral of the rope. Make the splice as follows:

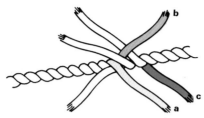

Unravel the strands for 7.5 cm on each end of the rope, and bring the two rope ends together, alternating the strands (a), (b) and (c) of the left-hand rope end with the strands in the right-hand rope end, as above.

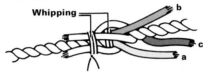

Tie light twine or whipping thread around the strands of both ends of the rope, as above, to keep rope from unravelling any farther as you work.

Working "uphill"—against the lay or spiral of the rope—begin splice by weaving and tucking each strand through, as above; repeat three times, always alternating them in the same sequence. Cut the whipping and turn the rope around. Finish the splice by weaving the remaining three strands of rope, following the same pattern.

Making an eye splice

An eye splice is formed by bending an end of rope back and splicing it into the rope so that the end of the rope becomes a loop. Such splices are used on boat mooring ropes, and to attach the stretcher dowel in a hammock to the hammock's harness ropes (see page 93). For a hammock, the first eye splice is made in one of the two ropes on the outside of the harness. In weaving a splice, you hold the rope just below the splice area and twist main or standing part clockwise. This opens the main part enough to tuck a strand through. Use a marlinspike to keep strands separated during the tuck, withdrawing it when the

strand is in place. Prepare to make the eye splice by unravelling the strands at the end of the rope for 7.5 cm, then doubling the rope back on itself to form a small loop.

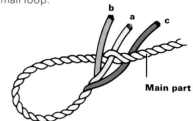

After twisting rope to open main part, tuck the first strand (a) through, uphill and against the spiral of the rope, as above. Position second and third strands (b) and (c) as shown.

Lift second strand (b) over main part of rope and tuck it into the lay of the rope, going "uphill" as before. Note that second strand (b) is inserted below first strand (a) and in a different part of the lay. At this stage the third strand (c) is underneath the main part.

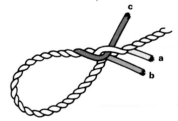

Turn loop over so that the third strand (c) now lies on top of main part, and tuck it in, doubling it under, as shown, to go against the lay. When this tuck is complete, turn loop over and begin a second three-step sequence with the first strand (a). Continue until all the loose strands of rope are woven into the main part. Trim any short ends close to rope.

Weaving, Braiding, Knotting
Making a Log Sling

For this project, you will need 60 cm of No. 8 (medium-weight) dyed cotton-duck canvas, 90 cm wide. It comes in many colours and may be purchased at a canvas, awning or tent shop. Cotton duck is weather-resistant, although some colours (notably reds) may fade in the sun. It may be washed with a mild detergent in warm water without affecting the colour. In addition to the tools listed on page 87, you will need the following from an awning shop, sailmaker or marine supply shop: 15 m of 10-ply waxed rayon twine; about 1.50 m of marline; and 5 m of 3-strand 1.5 cm terylene or manila rope. Note in Figure A that the selvedge—the woven edge that resists ravelling—is positioned at each of the narrow ends.

Pin the canvas to a flat working surface with weights or tacks. Then, with a yardstick, T-square and chalk, lay out and mark the cutting lines, the fold lines, the sewing lines, and the centre lines for the grommet holes. Mark the sewing lines on both sides of the canvas. Trim the canvas along the cutting lines with a large pair of shears. Crease the edges along the fold lines on each end for the hems, using the seam rubber to make sharp creases.

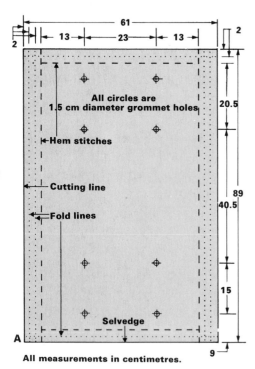

All measurements in centimetres.

Figure A: Use this pattern to make a canvas sling. Fold lines are shown by dots, sewing lines by dashes. All circles are grommet holes. Stitch grommets after canvas has been cut and hemmed.

A canvas sling makes a handy, comfortable means of hauling fireplace logs into the house; you might even want two so you could hold one in each hand. When not in use, the bright blue canvas with contrasting white grommets and stitches is attractive enough to be hung on a wall.

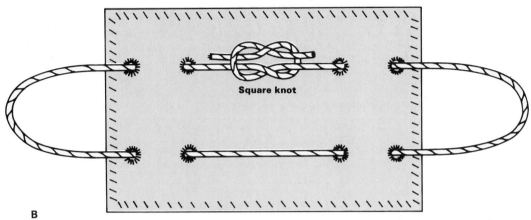

B

Figure B: To adjust the sling's handles to your height, run rope through completed grommets and tie the temporary square knot shown. If the sling hangs too low or too high when you lift it, adjust the knot. When length feels right, substitute a permanent short splice (page 89) for the knot.

Use a flat stitch along sewing lines to each corner and finish with a half-hitch (Craftnotes, page 88). Then make hems in both sides, overlapping at the corners (photograph 2). With a hammer and a 1.5 cm canvas punch, cut the eight grommet holes at the positions marked in Figure A. Stitch grommet rings around each hole (Craftnotes, page 88).

Adjust the handles of the log sling to suit your own height. When the grommets are finished, run the length of rope through the grommet holes, as shown in Figure B, so that the ends meet in the middle. Tie the ends in a square knot and bring together the two handles. The sling, even with a log in it, should hang comfortably at your side. If it drags on the ground, shorten the handles and re-tie the square knot. When the handles are the right length, substitute a permanent short splice (Craftnotes, page 89).

2: At each corner of the sling, overlap the two hems and stitch inside edges together. Tie a half-hitch to finish stitch and trim loose ends.

Weaving, Braiding, Knotting

Making a Naval Hammock

To make a rope-and-canvas hammock, you will need heavy No. 4 cotton duck, a good bit thicker than the medium-weight No. 8 canvas suggested for the log sling. About 2.5 m of 90 cm No. 4 duck will do for the hammock; an awning or tent shop or a sailmaker can supply it dyed or undyed. In addition to the tools shown on page 87, you will need 21 m of 1 cm terylene or manila rope; two oak dowels 103.5 cm long and 3 cm in diameter; two brass rings with 7.5 cm

Aboard ship there are usually plenty of strong supports that will hold a hammock. On land, use trees or posts spaced about 3 m apart for your hammock supports.

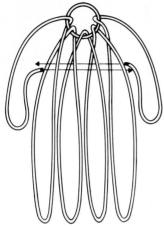

D

Figure D: To make the large clew (knot) in the harness ropes, turn four 1 m long loops over the brass ring. Twist ropes so the back and the front of the loops are reversed, then weave free ends of rope through as shown.

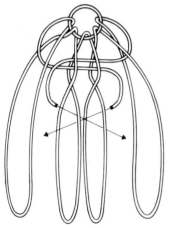

E

Figure E: As the second step in making the clew, by-pass the two outside loops and weave the free rope ends through two centre loops that you have twisted again in order to bring the rear of each centre loop forwards.

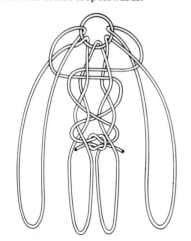

F

Figure F: As the final step in making the clew, reverse the direction of free rope ends as before and, again by-passing outer loops, weave through twisted inner loops once more. Tie off rope ends with the square knot shown.

outside diameters; a 30 m spool of 10-ply waxed rayon twine; and about 6 m of marline for stitching the 16 grommet holes and for lashing the outer harness ropes. Most large hardware shops stock rope and twine; the marline and the brass rings can be obtained from marine supply shops.

Follow the pattern (Figure C) to measure, mark and cut the canvas. Mark fold lines, binding and hem stitches, and grommet hole centres, using chalk of a colour that contrasts with the canvas. Mark the sewing lines on both sides of the canvas to help you keep the stitches aligned. Cut along the cutting line with large shears. Fold the canvas along the fold lines for the hems and use a seam rubber to press sharp creases. Sew both hems with flat stitches (Craftnotes, page 88) spaced at 6 mm intervals. Seal the hems with flat stitches at all four corners (photograph 2, page 91). Use the canvas punch to make holes for the 16 grommets, punching through the two layers of canvas in the hemmed areas. Sew grommets for all 16 holes (Craftnotes, page 88), stitching through both layers of canvas.

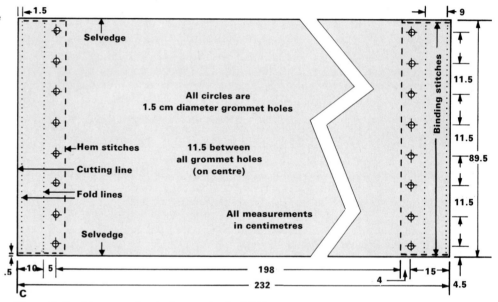

Figure C: On this pattern for the hammock, the fold lines are shown by dots, the sewing lines by dashes. Hems are flat-stitched through three thicknesses made by the two folds.

The harness and clew

For each end of the hammock, you must prepare a set of ropes called a harness. As illustrated on the left, these ropes are braided into a large knot which is called the clew, and is fastened to a brass ring (see colour photograph opposite and on pages 86 and 91).

To make the harness, hang a brass ring from a post and cut off a 9 m length of 1 cm manila rope. Hold one end of the rope with your foot (or have someone hold it for you) as you feed the other end through and around the ring five times; this will give you four loops of rope and two ends hanging from the ring (Figure D). Adjust ropes so that each loop and the two free ends of rope hang about a metre below the brass ring.

In turn, twist each of the loops to bring the back of the loop forward, weaving pattern, but this time by-pass the outside loop on each side (Figure E). the direction with both ends of rope and twisting the loops again, repeat the weaving pattern, but this time by-pass the outside loop on each side (Figure E). Make a third identical weave (Figure F), again by-passing the outside loops. Tighten the knot or clew you have just woven so that there is no slack in the weave, tie the two free ends with a square knot, and trim off the rope ends.

Near the bottom of each loop, cut the rope so the front piece will be slightly shorter than the back piece. Spread the ropes in a fan shape, with the longest sections on the outside, and the longer piece of each loop you have cut outside the shorter piece of the same loop.

A 103.5 cm long oak dowel across each end keeps the hammock from folding over you like a cocoon when you lie on it. Saw a notch about 3 mm deep in each end of each dowel, make a pencil mark every 11.5 cm along each length.

Make a single eye-splice loop on one of longest outside ropes (Craftnotes, page 89). Then lay harness and dowel on the floor, inserting one end of the dowel into the loop of the eye splice. In sequence, nail harness ropes to each pencil mark on the dowel (Figure G); these nails will be removed later, so drive them only part-way in. When all the ropes are stretched evenly, lift the harness by the metal ring. The dowel should hang horizontally, with no slack in any of the ropes. If any ropes are slack, remove temporary nails and make necessary adjustments. Repeat the procedure for the other harness.

The clew is a large knot braided into each set of harness ropes just below the brass rings from which the harness hangs. The two clews— one on each end—keep the harness ropes from snarling or chafing when the hammock swings.

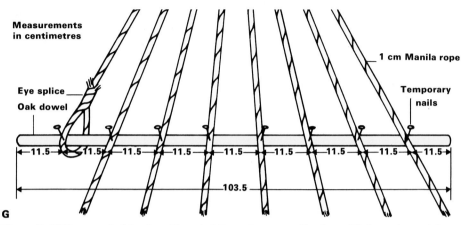

Measurements in centimetres

1 cm Manila rope

Eye splice
Oak dowel
Temporary nails

11.5 11.5 11.5 11.5 11.5 11.5 11.5 11.5 11.5

103.5

G

Figure G: With one end of the dowel inserted through an eye splice (page 89), lay out remaining seven ropes as shown and drive a 4 cm nail through each rope to hold it temporarily.

Each nail now marks the point where an eye-splice loop will be located. With the dowels still in place, double back the ends of the ropes and make eye splices (Craftnotes, page 89). Trim loose strands from the splice close to the main part of each rope. Remove all nails and set the spreader dowels aside. In sequence, insert the loops of the eye splices through each of the grommet holes in the canvas. Slide the dowels through the loops again (Figure H). To keep the hammock spread, lash the outside ropes of the harness to the ends of the dowels with marline, using the technique shown in photograph 3.

Now you are ready to hang your hammock. Tie the rings to posts or trees that are about 3 m apart. Leave plenty of slack in the middle; the centre of the canvas should hang 30 to 60 cm below the level of the rings on the harness. To use the hammock, sit sideways in the middle; then swing your feet up and over carefully until your weight is centred in the hammock. When you first try a hammock, the canvas may feel stiff; with use, it will loosen and conform to the shape of your body. You can speed this process by soaking it overnight in water. To clean your hammock, untie lashings, remove harnesses and spreaders, wash canvas in warm water with a mild detergent, then rinse and dry.

3: To keep ends of hammock spread, use a piece of marline, tying a square knot around the outer rope and lashing it to the end of the dowel as pictured. Then wrap a second piece of marline around the dowel over the first piece of marline and knot it in place.

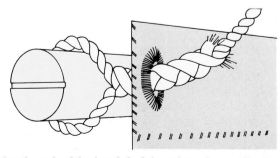

H

Figure H: After notching the ends of the dowel, feed them through eye-splice loops underneath the canvas hem at both ends of the hammock. The splices will fit snugly in the grommet holes.

HARDANGER EMBROIDERY
Scandinavian Handwork

By Marion Scoular

Hardanger, also known as Scandinavian embroidery, is characterized by geometric patterns formed with open squares and embroidered blocks. These effects are achieved by stitching over some fabric threads, while other threads are cut and withdrawn, as they are in other forms of drawn-thread embroidery.

Hardanger is named after a district in south-western Norway, where people use this form of embroidery to decorate household and personal linens. Embroidery artist Rita Tubbs' painstaking re-creation of an heirloom Norwegian costume is pictured below; it was copied from a costume left to her by her mother, a native of Namdalseid, Norway. Rita worked hardanger

This Norwegian costume is a replica of an authentic heirloom. The apron border, collar and cuffs have been worked in a particularly intricate design of classic white-on-white hardanger embroidery which gives a lace-like appearance to the even-weave linen.

embroidery on the collar and cuffs of the blouse and the border of the apron. Hardanger is traditionally worked in white thread on white even-weave linen as shown in the costume, in contrast to the silk on gauze used in an ancient form of white-on-white work done by the Persians. Although white thread on white fabric is still considered classic hardanger, colourful threads and fabrics began to be used in the early 19th century.

The geometric appearance of hardanger embroidery is created with embroidered blocks and cut-out squares that follow the fabric threads of an even-weave fabric.

Stitch key

Satin stitch

Woven bar

Vertical lace filling

Picot

Materials and basic preparation

Hardanger fabric with an even weave (having the same number of threads per centimetre horizontally and vertically) may be used for hardanger embroidery. In fact, you can order an even-weave cotton fabric called hardanger cloth from mail order firms. I used it for all of the projects that follow. In addition to the hardanger cloth, you need: a blunt size 22 tapestry needle; one ball No. 5 cotton perle thread for the satin stitch blocks, and one ball No. 8 cotton perle thread for the filling; and sharp-pointed embroidery scissors.

Three-step procedure

The geometric pattern of hardanger embroidery is accomplished in three separate steps (Craftnotes opposite). The first step is to embroider the satin stitch blocks. Photograph 1 (below) shows satin stitch blocks worked in a diamond shape. These blocks must be worked first because, apart from being decorative, they serve as a reinforcement for the ends of the threads that are cut out and withdrawn in the second step. Photograph 2 shows the same diamond motif with the threads cut out creating holes and exposed threads. The third step is to decorate the exposed threads with a needlewoven bar (photograph 3) and to decorate the holes with lace filling and picots, small loops which are made with the embroidery thread (photographs 4 and 5).

1: The first step in hardanger is to work the kloster or satin stitch blocks, 5 stitches over 4 threads each, placed here to form a diamond.

2: The second step is to cut and withdraw fabric threads, where they are supported by kloster blocks, creating holes and exposed threads.

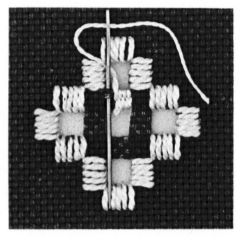

3: The third step is to decorate the exposed horizontal or vertical threads by weaving each group into a bar using the needleweaving stitch.

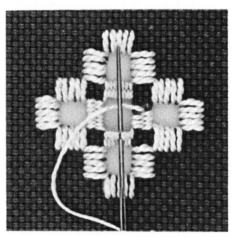

4: When you have woven to the middle of the fourth bar, pierce the centre of the previous bar to start a stitch called vertical lace filling.

5: This diamond motif has woven bars with vertical lace filling and picots, small loops made with the embroidery thread.

CRAFTNOTES: HARDANGER STITCHES

Hardanger embroidery is worked in three steps. The first step is to stitch the satin stitch blocks (Craftnotes, page 105), called kloster blocks, which outline the squares to be cut out, securing the ends of the cut thread. The blocks are stitched over an even number of fabric threads and are made up of the number of fabric threads plus one (usually 5 stitches over 4 threads). The second step is to cut the fabric threads. If vertical threads, called warp, are protected by a kloster block, then warp threads are cut leaving only horizontal threads called weft. If weft threads are protected, then weft threads are cut leaving only warp. If both warp and weft are cut, a hole is created. The third step is to decorate the threads exposed after cutting with woven bars, picots, and lace filling.

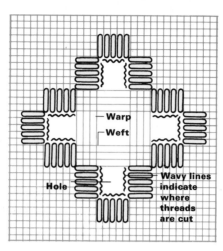

All threads to be withdrawn are cut before any are pulled out. On wrong side with embroidery scissors, snip threads at right angles to the kloster block supporting them (as shown above, along zigzag line). When all cut threads are withdrawn from the diamond motif, five holes are created. The hole in the centre is created by removing the warp threads from top to bottom and the weft from right to left.

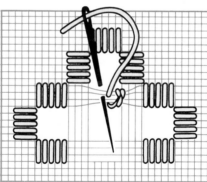

To decorate exposed fabric threads with a woven bar, use the needleweaving stitch. Place the needle under two fabric threads, then over two threads (above). See photograph 3, opposite.

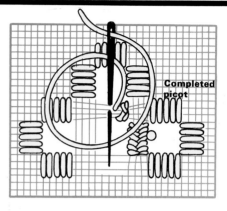

To make a picot, a small loop made with the embroidery thread, on a woven bar; needleweave to the centre of the exposed threads, then bring the thread around to the front and under the needle (above), and pull the needle through. Continue needleweaving until you reach the end of the bar.

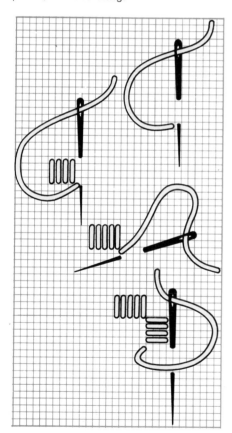

To stitch a kloster block, work 5 stitches over 4 threads (above). Make the stitches along the warp, if the warp threads are to be cut and withdrawn. If weft threads are to be cut and withdrawn, make stitches along weft. Complete all kloster blocks before cutting any threads.

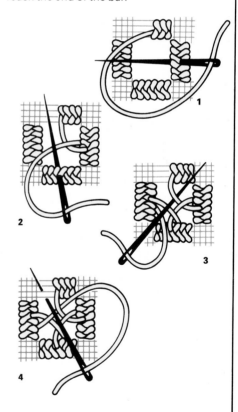

To fill the open areas with vertical lace, work to the middle of the fourth bar and make a stitch piercing the centre of the last bar completed (1 above). Continue around the four bars piercing the centre of each (2 and 3 above). Continue weaving the fourth bar (4 above). See photographs 4 and 5, opposite.

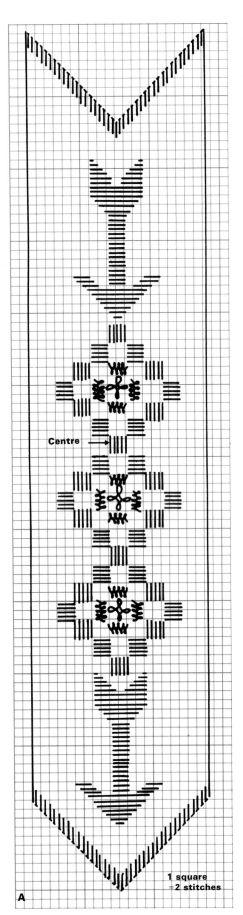

Centre →

1 square
=2 stitches

A

The centre three motifs of this bookmark are outlined with kloster blocks whose open spaces are worked with woven bars and lace filling; the arrows are worked in satin stitches.

Needlecrafts

A Bookmark

To make the bookmark pictured above, you need two pieces of hardanger cloth 7.5 by 25.5 cm. On one piece of fabric find and mark the centre. Following the diagram (left), and using No. 5 cotton perle thread, start stitching the first kloster block in the centre and work from the centre of the design down and then back up (Figure A). All blocks are five stitches over four threads. Complete all the kloster blocks (Craftnotes, page 97) for the three diamond-shaped motifs. The next step is to work the arrows in satin stitch also (see Craftnotes, page 105). The position of the arrow is shown in Figure A. When all the satin stitching is completed, cut and draw the threads (page 97). Using No. 8 cotton perle thread, work four woven bars with a vertical lace stitch (page 97) in the centre cut-out space of each motif.

To finish, place the embroidered fabric face down on the second piece of hardanger cloth. Tack the two pieces of fabric right sides together and machine-stitch approximately six threads away from the widest part of the design along the two long sides, thus forming a long tube. Trim the seams to 6 mm and turn the tube right side out. Press it lightly with a steam iron set on "cotton", laying the embroidery side face down on a towel. To finish each end, start at left edge and work a row of buttonhole stitches (Craftnotes, page 105) picking up four horizontal threads of the fabric for the first stitch. Then, working from left to right, descend one thread of the fabric with each stitch until the centre, then begin ascending one thread until the edge is reached. Trim the fabric close to the buttonhole stitch.

Figure A: The hardanger embroidery book mark shown on the left, is started at the centre kloster or satin stitch block, as indicated on this pattern, near the middle of the fabric.

Needlecrafts
A Cocktail Mat

As well as protecting a table top from being marked by glasses and bowls, cocktail mats can add a decorative note to any occasion. To work hardanger into a cocktail mat, as illustrated below, cut a piece of hardanger cloth 23 cm square. I like the contrast of the white stitches on bright red cloth, but the choice of colours is optional. Measure 11.5 cm in from the side to find the centre of the top edge of the fabric, and then from the centre, measure down 5 cm (Figure B, page 100). At this point, begin the satin stitch blocks (5 stitches over 4 fabric threads) that form the large diamond motif. Using No. 5 cotton perle thread, stitch the first block in vertical stitches, then a block of horizontal stitches; alternating blocks are worked clockwise to form a diamond (Figure B). The bottom stitch of the horizontal block and the first stitch of the vertical block share a hole.

The use of colour in hardanger embroidery creates a very striking effect, as shown in this red cocktail mat embroidered in white thread. The circles, stars and diamonds in the design, all made with straight stitches, show up vividly against the red background.

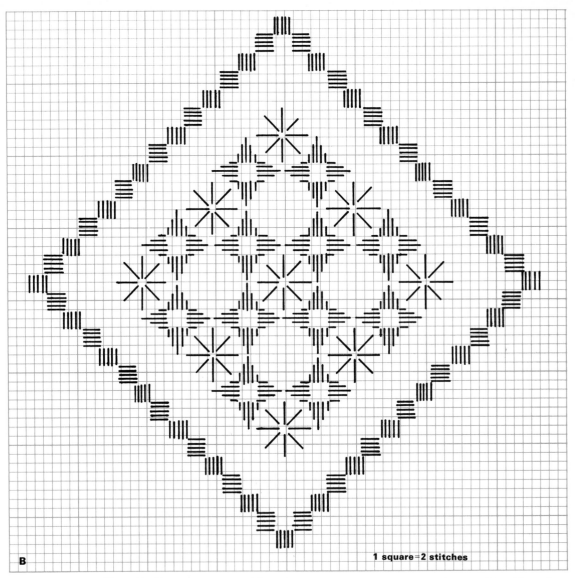

1 square = 2 stitches

B

Figure B: The satin stitches in this cocktail mat are varied in length so that the sides of four of them appear circular. Some of the circles are filled with stars made of 8 running stitches.

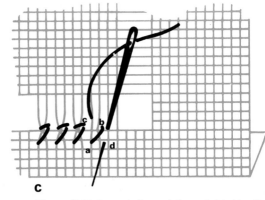

C

Figure C: To hemstitch, work from right side of fabric. Bring needle up 2 threads below openwork (a). Bring needle right to left (b to c) under 2 vertical threads; pull to front. Insert needle into hem from back, emerge on front 2 threads below openwork (d). Repeat across hem.

Start the star-like motif in the exact centre of the mat. Make 8 running stitches (see Craftnotes, page 105) from the centre point, each 5 threads long, to form a star. The satin stitches that surround the star are graduated lengths on either side of a long centre stitch to make the points shown. The centre stitch of each of these blocks is over 6 threads, the two stitches on either side of it are over 4 threads and the end stitches of each side are over 2 threads. To place the satin stitch blocks evenly around the star, count 8 threads from the centre point of the star and begin the longest stitch (over 6 threads) here. Follow diagram (above) for the position of the remaining stars and satin stitch blocks. When the embroidery is complete, carefully cut the threads inside the small squares formed by the graduated satin stitches.

To finish the edges with a hemstitched hem (an openwork finish), turn the raw edge to the wrong side of the fabric making the fold 6 mm from the raw edge. Tack the hem following the exact thread of the fabric. For an openwork of 2 threads, cut ends of 2 threads on each of the four sides directly above the folded raw edge and carefully pull them out. Hemstitching can be worked from left to right or right to left. Figure C shows hemstitch being worked from right to left. To fasten end of thread, after last hemstitch, hide the end of the thread in the hem and fasten with a few small stitches.

Needlecrafts
Wine Place Mat and Napkin

The dark red fabric provides an interesting background for the hardanger embroidery shown below. A detail of this place mat is shown on page 94. This type of embroidery is practical for a place mat and napkin set because, although it looks delicate, it withstands both machine washing and tumble drying on gentle cycles. To iron, place the dampened mat embroidery side down on a towel, then press with iron set on "cotton".

To make the place mat, cut a piece of hardanger cloth 33 by 46 cm. Using No. 5 cotton perle thread, begin the satin stitch blocks 3 cm in from the edge of the centre of the shorter side (Figure D, page 102). The last stitch of one block and the first stitch of the next block share a hole. The satin stitch bars in each of the four corners are 13 stitches over 4 threads. Work the kloster blocks along each of the four sides following the pattern (Figure D, page 102). There are 55 satin stitch blocks on each short side (not counting the corner bars), and 87 satin stitch blocks along each long side. When the outer row is completed and you have met the starting block, work the decorative inside row using a double running stitch (see Craftnotes, page 105). There should be eight fabric threads between the row of satin stitch blocks and the row of double running stitches.

This attractive place mat and napkin are co-ordinated with the same hardanger embroidery border design; the corner motif is more elaborate on the place mat.

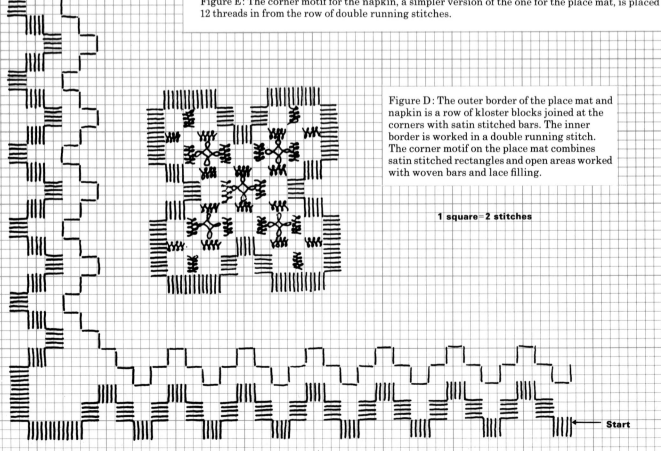

The motif in the lower right corner of the place mat is 12 threads above and 12 threads in from the double running stitch row. Start the outer satin stitch bars, which are 13 stitches over 4 threads, 12 threads above the uppermost double running stitch (Figure D). The inner satin stitch blocks are 5 stitches over 4 threads. After the satin stitch blocks are completed, the threads inside each block are cut and pulled. The threads that are exposed are worked with bars and lace filling (Craftnotes, page 97) following patterns indicated in Figure D.

To make the matching napkin, cut a piece of hardanger cloth 34 cm square. Begin the satin stitch blocks 3 cm in from the edge following the same pattern for the borders used for the place mat, except there will be 55 satin stitch blocks between the corner bars. A decorative row of double running stitch is placed 8 threads in from the satin stitch row. The corner motif (Figure E) is 12 threads in and 12 threads above the uppermost stitch of the double running stitch row. The motif is made up of five groups of 4 satin stitch blocks. The threads are cut from the centre of the five squares formed and only the middle square is worked with lace. To finish, turn raw edges under 6 mm and fold again to align with the same thread as the outermost satin stitches and hem.

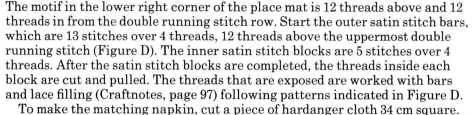

1 square
=2 stitches

E

Figure E: The corner motif for the napkin, a simpler version of the one for the place mat, is placed 12 threads in from the row of double running stitches.

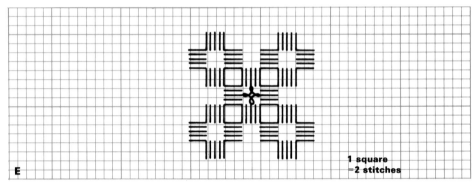

Figure D: The outer border of the place mat and napkin is a row of kloster blocks joined at the corners with satin stitched bars. The inner border is worked in a double running stitch. The corner motif on the place mat combines satin stitched rectangles and open areas worked with woven bars and lace filling.

1 square=2 stitches

← Start

102

D

White Place Mat and Napkin

By Rita Allgood Tubbs
This lovely place mat and napkin have been worked in the traditional
hardanger of white stitching on white fabric. The edging of Italian
hemstitching, a decorative openwork hem, and fringe, complement the
hardanger embroidery. The openwork for the hemstitching is cut and
withdrawn first, the hemstitching is worked next, and then the hardanger
embroidery is worked.

To make the place mat, cut a piece of hardanger cloth 36 by 46 cm. Since the
hemstitching is part of the design, it is easier to do it first, but the fringe is left
to last. Starting at the lower right corner, measure 2.5 cm in from the edge to
allow for fringe and pull out 1 thread (Figure F). Count 4 threads towards
centre and pull out the next thread. Now remove 3 threads on each side of this

The delicate beauty of traditional white hardanger embroidery worked on white even-weave
fabric is illustrated by this place mat and matching napkin.

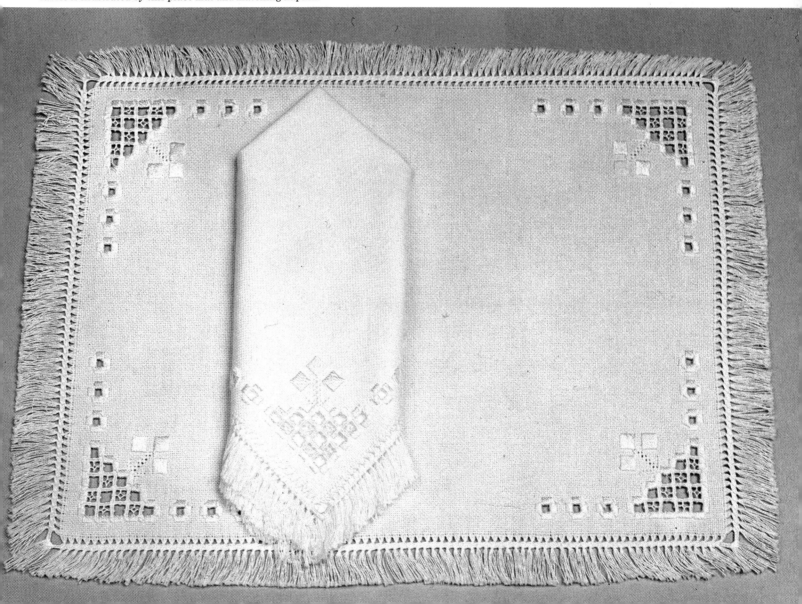

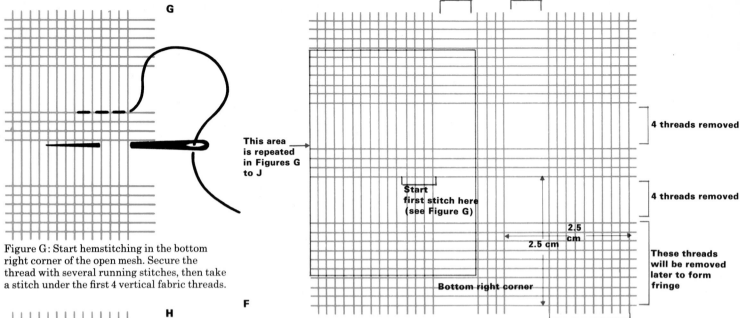

Figure G: Start hemstitching in the bottom right corner of the open mesh. Secure the thread with several running stitches, then take a stitch under the first 4 vertical fabric threads.

4 threads removed

This area is repeated in Figures G to J

4 threads removed

4 threads removed

Start first stitch here (see Figure G)

2.5 cm

2.5 cm

These threads will be removed later to form fringe

Bottom right corner

F

Figure F: To begin the hemstitching pictured on page 103, an open mesh 2.5 cm from the edge along each of the four sides is formed by withdrawing 4 threads from each side of a 4-thread group.

group of 4 threads. Repeat this procedure on each of the sides of the place mat, leaving an open mesh (Figure F). To begin hemstitching, fasten thread by taking a few running stitches in the fabric between the two spaces where the threads were withdrawn (Figure G). Insert the needle, right to left, under the first 4 threads in the lower space. Bind these 4 threads together by taking a stitch back over them, bringing the needle out in the upper space at the left of the same 4 threads (Figure H). Then bind them together in the upper space by taking a stitch back over them (Figure I) and bring the needle out again at the left of the same 4 threads in the upper space. Repeat the process, inserting the needle from right to left under the next 4 threads of the lower space (Figure J) and proceed as before, binding 4 stitches together first at the bottom and then at the top. At the corner (Figure K), weave a bar over the 4 horizontal threads (Craftnotes, page 97), and then buttonhole stitch (see Craftnotes opposite) around small woven square to turn corner. Next, turn the place mat so that the left side becomes the bottom and weave another bar (Figure K). Continue the hemstitching along each side. Do not pull remaining threads from

Figure H: To bind the four threads together at the bottom open mesh, take a stitch across them and bring the needle up at the upper edge of the horizontal 4-thread group.

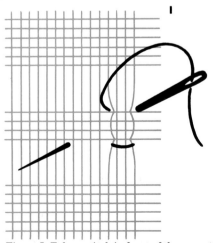

Figure I: Take a stitch in front of the same 4 threads (as in Figures G and H). Bring the needle out again at the top to the left of the threads to bind them together.

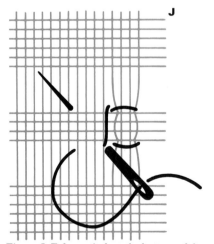

Figure J: Take a stitch at the bottom of the next group of 4 vertical threads to bind them together after bringing down the thread from the top of the previous group of 4 threads.

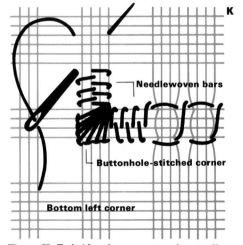

Figure K: To bridge the corner, work a needlewoven bar between hemstitching and corner, buttonhole stitch in corner, a needlewoven bar; then take a stitch over first 4 threads of left side.

Needlewoven bars

Buttonhole-stitched corner

Bottom left corner

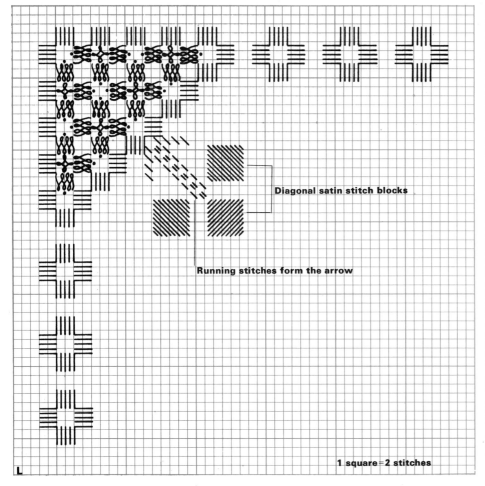

Diagonal satin stitch blocks

Running stitches form the arrow

1 square = 2 stitches

L

Figure L: This corner motif is repeated in each of the four corners of the white place mat but in only one corner of the matching napkin. The 3 diagonal satin stitch blocks and the arrow are worked after the kloster blocks, cutting, and lace filling are completed.

hemstitching to the edge of the fabric (to make the fringe) until the embroidery has been completed.

The place mat is now ready for the hardanger embroidery. Work the kloster blocks starting in the corner 8 threads up from the hemstitching. Make 5 satin-stitched blocks, 4 threads apart. Repeat this vertically, starting in 8 threads from the hemstitching on the left side and leaving 4 threads between blocks. To complete the third side of the triangle and the 3 squares on either side of the triangle, follow the klosters as indicated in Figure L. When all the kloster blocks are completed, carefully cut the threads from the 3 squares on either side of the triangle. Then carefully cut the threads from the squares that form the triangular motif.

To finish the embroidery, make woven bars of all the exposed threads in the triangle (Figure L), and stitch the picots shown (Craftnotes, page 97). Then work vertical lace filling in the squares as indicated. To complete the motif, make small diagonal running stitches over 2 threads in the shape of an arrow. The centre row of stitches is worked with a double thread. Work the three blocks shown in diagonal satin stitch. Embroider this motif in each of the four corners of the place mat.

To make the matching napkin, cut a piece of hardanger cloth 46 cm square. Hemstitch as you did the edge of the place mat (page 104). Make the same triangular corner design as for the place mat, but in one corner only. Finish both place mat and napkin by pulling out remaining threads of the marked-off 2.5 cm on each side between hemstitching and edge (Figure F). This will form the fringe and complete the project.

CRAFTNOTE ON BASIC STITCHES

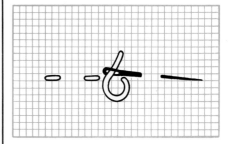

Running stitch: the stitches are of even length and equally spaced.

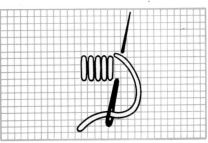

Satin stitch: close parallel stitches in line with fabric threads.

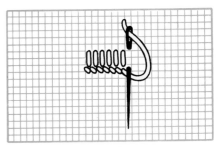

Buttonhole stitch: take needle through the yarn loop on each stitch.

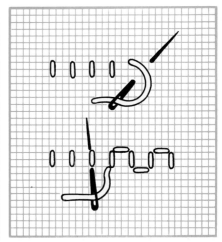

Double running stitch: even vertical stitches, returning horizontally.

HERALDRY

A Medieval Legacy

By William Metzig; J. P. Brooke-Little

Armorial bearings, the distinguishing marks borne by a medieval knight on his shield, were all that kept him from total anonymity within the heavy and cumbersome armour that covered him from head to toe. In battle, such anonymity could be fatal, since no one could know for sure if he were friend or foe and could hardly wait for an introduction.

The knight was not a legendary figure, but a real person, usually of noble birth, who was given land in return for military service to his feudal superior. To let the world know at a glance who he was, he first adopted insignia to mark his shield. Then, to add colour and dash to tournaments, he had his insignia embroidered on the coat, called a tabard or surcoat, that he wore over his armour to keep it from rusting in the rain and to keep himself cool in the sun. This flowing coat of decorated fabric was the original "coat armour" and the insignia became known as a "coat armour" as well.

Such symbols chosen by knights might demonstrate a simple colour and pattern preference, they might symbolize virtues and attributes, or they might even make a rebus—a word-picture of his name. But as more and more knights assumed armorial bearings, the possibility of confusion arose.

Medieval knights engage in battle, in armour protected by a fabric surcoat. This original "coat armour" at a later time would be decorated with the insignia here used only on the shields.

Enter the heralds

The dilemma was solved by the heralds, those messengers of kings who also graced the medieval scene as arrangers of tournaments, where the nobility displayed battle skills. By assuming responsibility for systematizing the design and execution of armorial bearings, so important to those trying to identify the participants in a tournament, they created the art and science that bears their name: heraldry. In many cultures since the beginnings of civilization, men have had symbols, badges and emblems to represent name,

Coats of arms are used not only by individuals but also by larger bodies, such as corporations or cities. The illustration opposite from the Ströl Heraldische Atlas, a German treatise on heraldry published in 1899, shows the arms of: 1, Amsterdam; 2, Oxford; 3, Brussels; 4, Schaffhausen (Switzerland); 5, Le Havre; 6, Murlo, and 7, Sorbano (Italy); 8, Leipzig; 9, Hanover; 10, Caslav (Czechoslovakia); 11, Maros-Vásárhely (Rumania); 12, Bombay.

1.

2.

FORTIS EST VERITAS

4

3.

5.

6.

7.

8.

9.

10.

11.

12.

URBS·PRIMA IN INDIS

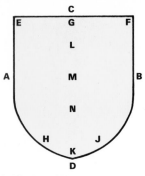

A

Figure A: The heraldic points on a shield are indicated by letters; they are described in heraldic terminology as follows:

A: Dexter side (shield carrier's right).
B: Sinister side (shield carrier's left).
C: Chief (top of the shield).
D: Base (bottom of the shield).
E: Dexter chief (top left).
F: Sinister chief (top right).
G: Middle chief (top centre).

H: Dexter base (bottom left).
J: Sinister base (bottom right).
K: Middle base (bottom centre).
L: Honour point (one-quarter down centre line).
M: Fess point (half-way down centre line).
N: Nombril point (three-quarters down centre line).

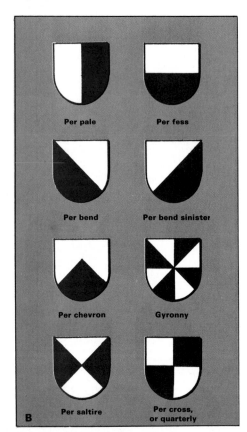

B

Per pale   Per fess
Per bend   Per bend sinister
Per chevron   Gyronny
Per saltire   Per cross, or quarterly

Figure B: The shield is referred to as the field—the area on which the design is drawn. Medieval field divisions are shown with their heraldic designations. Patterns that can be derived from these divisions are shown opposite in Figure C.

family or rank. Many of these symbols were incorporated into heraldic design. The eagle is a good example: it has been used by empires, monarchies, and republics. What distinguishes heraldry from ancient custom is, first, its systemization under heralds; and second, the custom that evolved whereby sons used the arms of their fathers.

The College of Arms in England, established in 1484 by Richard III, exists to this day and still carries the prestige of former times, deciding who is entitled to wear what coat of arms. Shakespeare's "Enter the heralds with trumpets" is a stage direction that probably gave rise to popular belief that heralds were trumpeters. Perhaps it was an economy measure in Elizabethan times to have actors double as heralds and trumpeters, but in fact the original heralds might have led in the trumpeters but never actually blew the trumpets.

The language of heraldry

The old French word for trumpet is *blazon*; and it was the blazon that announced the knights in their colours, bearing and wearing their coat of arms and ready to enter the tournament games. From this is derived the terms *emblazon*, meaning to depict an armorial design graphically, and *blazon*, to describe the design verbally. Blazonry is the language of medieval heraldry. A glossary on page 110 defines heraldic terms.

From shield to trade mark

I have no doubt that a knight visiting the 20th century in a time machine would be puzzled to see the wealth of commercial objects that bear coats of arms. What possible connection could he make between his medieval peers and a bottle of ginger ale, or a packet of cigarettes or a car? Remnants of heraldry would surround him in frivolous proliferation. Today coats of arms are used by states, churches, associations, universities and corporations; they may appear on notepaper, cars, jewellery and, by special permission, displayed in shops and stores.

The granting of arms was, and in some places still is, a serious custom. In England, the right to have such insignia has been controlled by the College of Arms for hundreds of years. During the 16th and 17th centuries, heralds were sent around the counties on missions known as the "Visitations", to record the arms and pedigree of the gentry. Heraldry, outside England and Scotland, is no longer under such rigid controls. But a study of its medieval origins offers insights into a remarkable culture of the past that was destroyed by the invention of gunpowder.

Medieval heraldic design

The shield was the field upon which the original armorial bearings were designed. For this reason, the shield remains the focal point today and is the only essential part of a coat of arms in contemporary designs. To understand the heraldic system, look first at the shield itself on which specific points are designated (Figure A). The dexter side corresponds to the right side of the shield carrier and the observer's left (hence the word dextrous). Figure B, left, illustrates the ways in which a field could be divided. At first glance, the medieval expressions for these divisions seem like pure nonsense to us; and in fact, it is a kind of medieval jargon; but the meanings are simple and merely indicate direction. Anyone who becomes seriously interested in heraldry would have to learn these words and expressions since they are used to describe, or blazon, coats of arms in a particular way. But the terms can also be read and savoured as evocations of a gallant, if barbarous, civilization of long ago. The heraldic language defined on this and the following pages will also be useful to crossword puzzle enthusiasts.

The honourable ordinaries

The geometric patterns opposite (Figure C) were called "honourable ordinaries" because they were used frequently, but with distinction. They are the oldest, simplest, and most basic patterns in heraldry. A glance at Figure B, left, shows how these patterns emerged when the shield was divided.

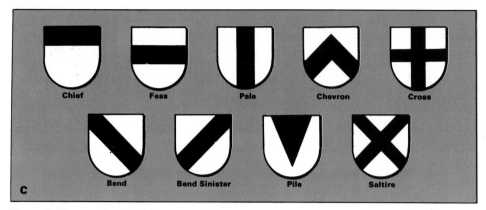

Figure C: These medieval shield patterns are called the honourable ordinaries in heraldic parlance.

The subordinaries

Scholars of heraldry dispute the actual number of subordinaries, a more intricate group of patterns that evolved to give distinction to coats of arms. Some say there are 14, others count more than 20 with all the variations. On the right are major subordinary patterns that all agree upon.

Representational patterns

Mythological beasts, animals, birds, plants, planets, the sun, tools, sailing ships, musical instruments, in short almost anything with a significant meaning for an individual, a family, or a nation may be considered a suitable design—called a charge—for a shield, so long as it retains a certain amount of dignity. Some of the oldest charges are shown below. Some of the varied positions assumed by heraldic animals are demonstrated by the six lions; English, Norwegian, Danish, Finnish, Spanish and Flemish royal families all adopted the lion as their emblem. Hereditary aspects of heraldry are indicated by the marks (Figure F) that sons placed upon a father's shield to make it their own. The labels in these charts are defined in the glossary, page 110.

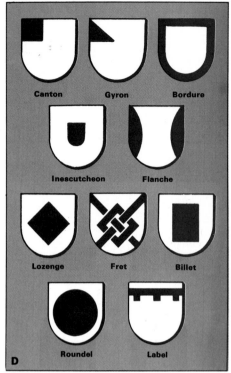

Figure D: The subordinaries are shield patterns, more complex and varied than the ordinaries illustrated on the left. They are equally esteemed in traditional heraldry.

Figure E: These are but a few of the many possible representational patterns, the pictorial designs called "charges" in heraldry. Unfamiliar heraldic terms used in the designations, many in Norman French, are defined in the glossary on page 110.

Figure F: Distinguishing marks assigned to sons to indicate birth rank in a family are called marks of cadency. Each son placed one on his father's shield to make it his own.

Glossary of Heraldic Terms

Achievement: A fully emblazoned coat of arms including shield, helmet, crest, mantling and motto (see Figure I).

Affrontée: Position displaying full face or front.

Annulet: A ring, symbol of the fifth son.

Armigerous: Arms-bearing.

Caboshed or Cabossed: Beast's head shown affrontée (see above) with no part of the neck included.

Cadency: Symbols for the first nine sons of a family, shown in Figure F.

Caduceus: Two snakes entwined on a staff, called the Rod of Hermes, symbol of a herald; also commonly used to describe the Rod of Aesculapius, symbol of a physician.

Caltrap: Medieval spur-like weapon having four spikes.

Charge: Medieval term for a pattern or symbol on a shield.

Clarion: A symbol of music.

Cockatrice: Mythical beast with the head of a cock and a dragon's tail, wings and feet.

Compartment: Area below the shield on which the supporters (see below) stand.

Couchant: An animal position, lying down, breast to earth and head raised.

Crescent: Crescent moon, horns turned inward; symbol for a second son (see Figure F).

Crest: Any decoration borne on the helm, like a plume or an animal.

Cross Moliné: Symbol for the eighth son.

Displayed: Bird viewed from the front with wings and legs outspread.

Dragon: Mythical creature, part bird, part beast, part reptile.

Embowed: Bent, or curved, like a bow.

Escutcheon: Another word for a shield, sometimes used to express an entire coat of arms.

Fleur-de-lis: Literally, flower of the lily, also called "flower of Louis" (XIV), the symbol of France, also the symbol of a sixth son.

Griffon: Mythical beast, half eagle, half lion.

Garb: A sheaf of corn or wheat.

Gaze: "At gaze," applied to a deer standing still and looking earnestly outwards.

Hatchment: A funeral achievement displayed on a diamond-shaped lozenge.

Helm: The knight's helmet.

Knight: Title of honour conferred for services performed in war (medieval).

Label: Mark of the first son and heir.

Mantling: Drapery flowing from beneath the wreath, covering the armour.

Martlet: Mythical legless bird, symbol of the fourth son because he inherits no land to light on.

Mullet: Five-pointed star; symbol of the third son.

Naiant: Fish in swimming position.

Octofoil: An eight-leaved flower; symbol of the ninth son.

Passant: An animal in a walking position.

Pennon: Small flag borne on the end of a lance.

Plenitude: Full, as "moon in plenitude"

Proper: Said of a charge (see above) appearing on the shield in its natural colours.

Rampant: An animal position—erect with hind paw on ground, three paws and tail raised.

Reguardant: An animal looking towards the sinister (right) side of the shield.

Rose: Symbol often associated with England; also symbol of the seventh son.

Salient: Animal's position, springing forward.

Séjant: Seated position.

Semée: Sprinkled, as "semée of fleur-de-lis" meaning that a shield is covered with that design.

Supporters: Figures flanking a shield, either animal or human.

Tierced in pairle: A shield divided into three equal portions.

Torse: Another word for wreath.

Trefoil: Three-leaved plant.

Unicorn: Mythical beast, like a horse, with cloven hoofs, a goatee and one horn in the centre of his forehead.

Volant: flying.

Winged: Said of a beast whose wings are coloured differently than its body.

Wivern: Mythical beast resembling a dragon with a knotted tail.

Wreath: A circlet of two-coloured silk placed on the helm and around the crest.

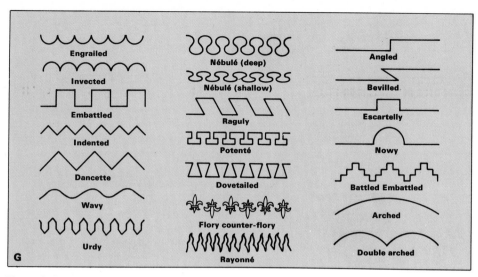

Figure G: Decorative lines of partition may be used to divide or outline any area of the shield.

The coat of arms of the King of France in the 17th century displays the ermine of royalty. The two shields, side by side, show the golden fleur-de-lis of King Louis XIV, on the left, and the arms of Navarre.

Lines of partition

Areas of heraldic design may be defined graphically by straight lines or by decorative lines like those shown above (Figure G). Some have symbolic meaning. For example, a wavy line may signify water, as in the coat of arms of the City of Paris (right), while the nebule, an old French word for "cloudy", is often used to indicate an uncertain past.

Tinctures: colours, metals and furs

Heraldic colours—clear, strong and brilliant—were originally chosen to give instant recognition on the battlefield (Figure H, below). Pastel colours are almost never used, even today. Other colours are used only when something is "rendered proper", that is, in its actual colours. The system of indicating colour by means of black-and-white dots and cross-hatching was invented by an Italian in the 17th century. Knowing the system, if you look at an old engraving of a coat of arms, you learn to read its colours from these patterns.

Furs, now rarely used, often indicated royalty as in the 17th-century arms of the King of France (above right). Some scholars think that in the original story of Cinderella, her slippers were actually of vair—squirrel fur—but the word was misread as *verre*, the French word for glass, giving rise to the legend.

In medieval times, one simple rule governed the use of all these tinctures: colour never lay on colour, nor metal on metal, nor fur on fur. Even today, when this rule is observed, clarity of the design is ensured.

The City of Paris added the cap on the staff to its coat of arms after the French Revolution. The arms of cities and towns in France that retained the fleur-de-lis did so on a grant from the Republic to connote a good city.

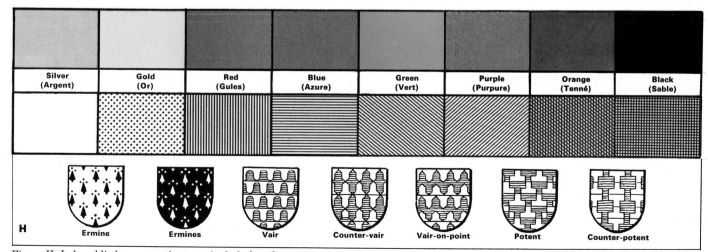

Figure H: In heraldic language, tinctures include furs (bottom row) as well as colours and metals (top rows). The heraldic word for each colour is given in parentheses. The black-and-white graphic equivalent below each colour block is used to represent that colour in an engraving.

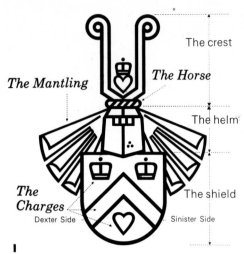

I

Figure I: A coat of arms is referred to as a "full achievement" when it has all the elements identified above. To this may also be added a motto and supporters—figures flanking the shield, as the lion and unicorn shown at right in the British Royal coat of arms.

Some European heraldic agencies

Austria: Heraldisch-Genealogische Gesellschaft
Adler, Vienna II, Haarhof 4a

Denmark: Statens Heraldiska Konsulent
Indenrigsministeriet
Kristiansborgs Slotsplads 1
DK-1218 Copenhagen K

England: College of Arms
Queen Victoria Street, London E.C.4

France: Président de la Société Française d'Héraldique et de Sigillographie,
60 rue des Francs-Bourgeois, Paris 3e

Germany: Herolds-Ausschuss der "Deutschen Wappenrolle",
1 Berlin 33 (Dahlem), Archivstrasse 12-14.
Genealogisch-Heraldische Gesellschaft,
34 Göttingen, Theaterplatz (Stadtarchiv)

Holland: Centraal Bureau voor Genealogie,
Nassaulaan 18, The Hague

Ireland: Chief Herald and Genealogical Officer,
Office of Arms, Dublin Castle, Dublin

Luxembourg: Délégué aux Relations Exterieures du Conseil Héraldique,
25 Rue Bertholet, Luxembourg

Norway: Head Archivist, Riksarkivet,
Bankplassen 3, Oslo 1

Poland: Archiwum Główne Akt Dawnych,
Warsaw ul. Długa 7

Scotland: Court of the Lord Lyon, H.M.
Register House, Princes Street, Edinburgh

Sweden: Riksarkivet, Munkbron II,
Stockholm 2

The parts of a coat of arms

Figure I shows how a coat of arms is assembled with its customary components. As I have mentioned, the shield is the only element that is essential. Other parts are basically decorative, though crest, position of helm, and colours are subject to control. The helm, of course, is the medieval helmet, and though it has little relevance to modern times it is retained as a traditional design element. The crest is borne on the helm, sometimes as a plume or as an heraldic bird or animal. As you will see on pages 114 and 115 the crest can be designed to suit an individual. The wreath or torse is a circlet representing two coloured silks, traditionally the principal colours of the shield; it tops the helm and encircles the base of the crest. Knights wore them to cover the joint between crest and mantling. The mantling is the drapery flowing from beneath the wreath symbolizing the knight's surcoat. Supporters are usually heraldic animals flanking the shield, but they may also be human figures. They stand on a ground called a compartment. The motto, originally a war cry, may express any dignified sentiment, belief or goal.

The British Royal insignia is properly displayed only by the Queen. The shield at centre is quartered to show (top left and bottom right) the golden lions of Richard the Lionheart and symbols for Scotland (top right) and Ireland (bottom left) held together with a blue garter signifying the Knights of the Garter, England's highest order of knighthood.

How heraldic designs develop

In 1198, Richard I (the Lionheart) assumed a striking coat of arms of three golden lions on a red shield. When Scotland and Ireland were added to the British realm, the shield was quartered and the emblems of these nations added. Richard's lions now occupy the first and third quarters of the British Royal Arms pictured above. The encircling garter bearing the words *Honi soit qui mal y pense* (Evil to him who evil thinks) was added as the result of a capricious incident in British history. At a celebration following the capture of Calais, the Countess of Salisbury dropped her blue garter. In a gesture of gallantry, Edward III wrapped it around his left knee and responded with the now famous phrase. He founded the Order of the Garter in 1348 and took this unusual emblem as its symbol.

Today the Queen's coat of arms bears the lion and the unicorn as supporters and the motto *Dieu et Mon Droit* (God and my right) which proclaims the divine right of kings. In English heraldry, only nobility and certain orders of knights are permitted to have supporters on their insignia. Outside England, however, supporters holding the shield are used freely.

Heraldic customs developed and spread over western Europe. Pictured opposite is part of a 17th-century board game whose purpose was to teach children of the Neapolitan nobility the coats of arms of their royal houses, vivid proof of the importance attached to heraldry at that time.

Coats of arms of 17th-century Neapolitan nobility spiral from the centre of this antique board game, once intended as an enjoyable means of instructing children about the glories and splendours of noble birth.

Know your heraldic rights

There is surely something satisfying, if not exciting, in knowing that you have an historical past, and the discovery that you are entitled to bear the coat of arms of an ancestor is stimulating proof. However, it is not easy proof to establish. Companies that offer to send a family coat of arms for a few pounds mislead many people into believing that the insignia they receive in the mail are actually their own. The standard texts on heraldry that these companies consult list thousands of family coats of arms dating back hundreds of years. Your name may be among them, but that is not proof that you are descended from that particular branch of that particular family. Should you bear the aristocratic old English name of Howard, for example, you are not necessarily entitled to assume the insignia of the Duke of Norfolk, head of the house of Howard. The Howard family tree had many branches, some with its own insignia and many without any, so it is a family, rather than a name, that one must be sure of. There are numerous heraldic agencies in Europe (see listing opposite) but they cannot really assure you of your right to a coat of arms unless you supply them with a detailed genealogy proving your lineage.

Heraldry in Britain today

To be entitled to bear a coat of arms in the United Kingdom, you must establish your direct, male line descent from someone to whom arms were once granted or allowed. If you cannot do this, however, you can petition for a new coat of arms to be granted to you. If you are a person of some distinction —a respectable, and probably fairly affluent citizen—your petition will be considered and is unlikely to be refused.

In England and Northern Ireland you would petition the Earl Marshal of England. He issues a Warrant to the Kings of Arms (the senior heralds) directing them to grant you such arms "as they shall think fit and proper". Ancient heraldic terminology is still used in modern heraldry.

In Scotland you would petition Lyon King of Arms, in Edinburgh, and he would grant the arms. Although the Scottish and English Kings of Arms grant arms, they do so with the authority of the Crown, for bearing arms is an honour and so stems from the Crown, which is the "Fount of Honour".

In the Republic of Ireland petitions are addressed to and grants of arms are made by the Chief Herald of Ireland, whose office is in Dublin Castle.

The coat of arms of the United States is called the Great Seal of the United States of North America. It is described in the records of the Continental Congress in heraldic language: "The escutcheon (*shield*) is composed of the Chief (*top of shield*) and Pale (*bottom of shield*) ... The latter represents the several states all joined in one solid compact entire, supporting a Chief, which unites the whole and represents Congress; the Motto alludes to this union. The Colours or tinctures of the Pale are those used in the flag of the United States; White signifies purity and innocence; Red, hardiness and valour. The Chief denotes Congress—Blue is the ground of the American uniform and this colour signifies Vigilance, Perseverance and Justice ... The escutcheon being placed on the Breast of the eagle displayed is a very ancient mode of bearing and is truly imperial ..."

Can you start anew?

Britain is the only country in Europe where heraldry is still protected by the law: if somebody bears arms in England or Scotland without authority, legal action may even be taken against him—although this has only occurred once in the last 200 years—in 1954.

In continental Europe, the heraldic scene is less formal. Although there were once heraldic authorities in most European countries, few now remain, and the use of arms is generally a matter of personal choice. These heraldic authorities mainly concern themselves with the arms of the nobility and of corporations. This means that in most of Europe, anybody can make up his own coat of arms and use it. However, such a coat of arms should not be too similar to an existing noble coat, for even if not illegal, it would be rather pretentious. Besides, it is more interesting and challenging to create an entirely unique and personal coat of arms.

Designing your own arms

Even if you are not allowed to display a personally designed coat of arms, as in Britain, anybody who wishes may experiment in heraldic design; for this is a fascinating mixture of art, craft and science. It is both amusing and instructive to design arms for real and fictional people. Enthusiasts have done this over the centuries, devising arms for pre-heraldic historical characters, biblical persons and saints, and characters in plays, operas and novels. Such arms are understood to be fictitious and their use in certain contexts is

An azure glove, appliquéd in red and trimmed in ermine, is prominent on the coat of arms of a glove maker. Four blue circles, called roundels, are decorated with golden mullets.

The family name Fantasia is rendered in this coat of arms as a golden bird of Paradise, or a fantasy. The family's Italian origin is shown by the Italian flag in centre of the crest.

The city of Noto on the coast of Sicily is depicted in this coat of arms for a physician named DiNoto. The caduceus, the symbol of the medical profession, is drawn on the ship's sail in the crest.

This coat of arms was designed for a man named Zak, which means young student in Russian. The shield gives the name pictorially by showing a student standing between two saplings and holding an open book in each hand.

The coat of arms of this husband and wife combines occupations of both families. The husband's family, once wheel-makers, now manufactures gears and tyres, shown by the half-wheel in the shield. The sheaf of wheat symbolizes the wife's farmer ancestors.

The name Shaeffer means shepherd and is indicated on this shield by golden sheep on a green field. The silver shepherd's shears further symbolize the occupation.

accepted: for example, churches often display arms which are attributed to their heavenly patron.

People who live in America, France, Germany, Holland, Sweden and many other European countries may, if they have not inherited arms, design them for their personal and family use.

The essence of good heraldry is that it should be simple, symbolic and have a definite visual impact. To achieve this, time-honoured symbols are employed and are depicted and disposed in conventional colours, forms and patterns. A good design has both a meaning and an intrinsic beauty.

The designer of arms has two vehicles for the display of heraldic symbols; the shield, which is a flat surface, and the helm, on which the crest is modelled in the round. A good designer will, therefore, try to conceive a crest which could be carved in wood and fixed to the helm. Obviously, before putting pen to paper, you should decide what you want to symbolise or illustrate.

Some ideas for heraldic design

The arms on this page, which were designed for people in Europe and America who had very different backgrounds and occupations, will serve to give some idea as to what can be symbolized. The captions explain the symbolism.

A husband and wife named Zahn-Narr are represented in this coat of arms by two shields conjoined. The profession of the husband, Zahn, a pharmacist, is represented in the crest at left by a caduceus in a mortar. The wife's crest, a jester, is "narr" in German. Her shield is decorated with a lyre, a musical symbol relevant to her background.

If the name or profession of the person for whom arms are being designed, are not readily translatable into symbolic form, what can be done? Fortunately, the things which can be symbolized in coats of arms are numerous and diverse. People may commemorate their favourite sport or pastime; their country, district or town of origin; a family tradition, or an esteemed quality or virtue; membership of a religious, social or ethnic group; the heraldry of families from which they have descents through females; the heraldry of their places of education—the possibilities are endless.

Other than in Scotland, where mottoes are granted, anyone may adopt a motto, even in England. It is usually depicted in a scroll beneath the arms, but is sometimes placed over the crest. If two mottoes are used, the one over the crest is normally a war cry. Mottoes range from elegant Latin quotations from the classics, to simple, even humorous puns on a surname.

Kloke means bell and Engel means angel, so the name portrayed is Kloke-Engel. Both are given equal prominence in this design created for a husband and wife.

This coat of arms was designed for a printer whose name, Schoenberg, means beautiful mountain. The name is depicted in the crest at the top as a mountain covered with flowers. The shield describes the printer's trade by the ancient symbol of the mythical griffon holding two printer's tools over an open book.

HERBS

For Flavour, Fragrance and Fun

By Mrs. A. DeCiantis; Marilyn Ratner

Herbs have always been prized for their many uses, ranging as far as the magic of witches' brews, but today it is the culinary and fragrant properties of herbs that we particularly appreciate. Gardeners and non-gardeners alike use such culinary herbs as sage and thyme to add flavour to food. Fragrant herbs like lavender are used in aromatic bouquets, pot-pourris, sachets, herbal shampoos, perfumes and oils. A number of herbs, such as the artemesias, are valued simply for their decorative appearance, while still others are used to make dyes and medicines. In ancient times, most medicines came from herbs, which originated largely in hot, dry lands with rather poor soil. Today, some are still credited with medicinal value but much of the old advice seems fanciful in light of modern knowledge. A Victorian cure for asthma, we are told, was to "mince garlic, spread it on thin bread and butter, and eat before going to bed". Many such examples fill pages of old herbals, early books detailing the practical uses of plants.

Many people first become interested in growing herbs for their food flavouring value. Then they may turn to growing herbs for fragrance or just because of their beauty, or to use them for something specific like dyeing.

What is a herb?

There is no precise way to define a herb. To a botanist, a herb is any herbaceous plant—one whose stem dies down to the root when winter comes. Herbaceous plants can be annual, biennial, or perennial; they include not only mint, parsley and anise, but peonies and potatoes. (By contrast, shrubs and trees are called woody plants because they have stems and branches that live on year after year.) To a herb enthusiast, however, herbs are all those plants—woody as well as herbaceous—whose leaves, flowers, seeds and other parts are especially valued for flavour, fragrance, dyeing or medicinal use.

Herbs are among the easiest plants to grow so this hobby can be enjoyed on many levels. If you are a beginner, you can start with one or two plants or a tiny garden, indoors or outdoors, and discover the taste and appearance of culinary herbs and the different ways one herb may be used. Sweet woodruff, for example, can flavour May wine or be dried for use in fragrant pot-pourris and wreaths. Parsley and basil go into pesto sauce for pasta (recipe on page 126). Fresh rosemary is known as the herb of remembrance, so it is particularly appropriate for use in gift baskets (page 124); it is a treat for the eye as well as for the taste buds, and if you like, you can grow it indoors in a hanging basket (page 122).

Experienced gardeners might choose to cultivate herbs of historical significance: for example, specialized herbs such as those used by the American Indians, or those described by Shakespeare. In designing a herb garden, examples from the past can be inspiring if one wants a lovely formal garden containing paths and geometric flowerbed shapes. One type is the 16th-century English knot garden which has a central knot of clipped herbs interlaced with one another, resembling a knotted rope. Another popular design is a cottage garden where the herbs are arranged close at hand for the convenience of the housewife. There is no need to have a formal garden unless you want to give it a lot of your time. You may prefer a simple and practical garden, requiring minimum care.

The following projects will acquaint you with a variety of herbs and ways to use them. Keep in mind that growing and enjoying herbs does not have to be time-consuming and complicated—but it can be fun.

This kitchen garden is situated conveniently by the back door so that culinary herbs can be gathered quickly for any meal. Fragrant and dye herbs occupy a separate bed near by.

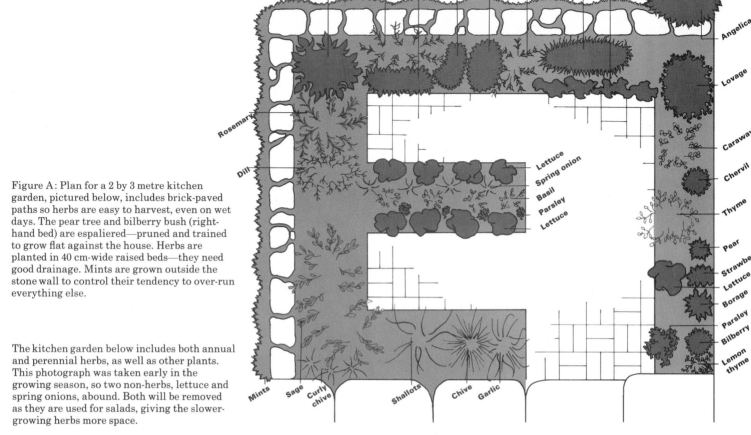

Mints · French sorrel · Summer savory · Oregano · Marjoram · Burnet · Winter savory · Tarragon · Lettuce

Angelica

Lovage

Rosemary

Caraway

Dill

Chervil

Lettuce
Spring onion
Basil
Parsley
Lettuce

Thyme

Pear

Strawberry

Lettuce

Borage

Parsley

Bilberry

Lemon thyme

Mints · Sage · Curly chive · Shallots · Chive · Garlic

Figure A: Plan for a 2 by 3 metre kitchen garden, pictured below, includes brick-paved paths so herbs are easy to harvest, even on wet days. The pear tree and bilberry bush (right-hand bed) are espaliered—pruned and trained to grow flat against the house. Herbs are planted in 40 cm-wide raised beds—they need good drainage. Mints are grown outside the stone wall to control their tendency to over-run everything else.

The kitchen garden below includes both annual and perennial herbs, as well as other plants. This photograph was taken early in the growing season, so two non-herbs, lettuce and spring onions, abound. Both will be removed as they are used for salads, giving the slower-growing herbs more space.

Planning your first herb garden

You can have a delightful herb garden the first season, but if you are a beginner, keep it small and simple. It will probably take three years before you are satisfied. There is no limit to the herbs you might include and the ways you could design your garden. What you grow should be determined by what you are going to use. For instance, if you like French food you might grow chervil and shallots. Italian food enthusiasts would include basil and oregano. Your local library will have reference books with simple instructions, and many books include garden designs as well as step-by-step growing information.

Do not begin on too large a scale. You can have a productive outdoor herb garden in a space no larger than 30 cm square. Start with a small variety of plants, repeat those you like best next year and add a few more, and so on. If you do not like something, do not grow it again. The chart on pages 127 and 128 has suggestions for beginners, but it is by no means complete. Consult other sources of horticultural information, such as your local garden club, for more information about herbs.

A garden like the one pictured opposite, located just outside the kitchen door, is often called a salad garden. To make a salad, you just pull some greens, snip some salad burnet (which has a fresh cucumber taste), cut a few culinary herbs, and you are nearly ready to eat. When you make breakfast, you can snip some chives or chervil to give a gourmet touch to a simple omelette.

Herbs do not have to be planted in a separate garden. It is fine to mix vegetables and herbs in the same area. In fact, herbs are often planted among vegetables, since their aroma seems to repel insects. Herbs can also occupy a sunny corner of a flower garden or edge a path leading across a lawn. In the garden shown here, fragrant herbs, used in pot-pourris, and dye herbs grow separately in a corner of the yard behind the house. They are planted in front of a stone wall that forms a natural border (photograph below).

Herbs popular in Shakespeare's day, and their Latin names

Bay
Laurus nobilis

Box
Buxus sempervivens

Broom
Cytisus scoparius

Burnet
Sanguisorba minor

Chamomile
Anthemis nobilis

Flax
Linum perrene

Heartsease
Viola tricolor

Hyssop
Hyssopus officinalis

Lavender
Lavandula vera

Lemon balm
Melissa officinalis

Marigold
Calendula officinalis

Rue
Ruta graveolens

Samphire
Crithmum martimum

Summer savory
Satureia hortensia

Tansy
Tanacetum vulgare

Thyme
Thymus serpyllum

Fragrant and dye herbs grow separately in their own garden where their grey, green, and silver shades intermingle. Included are foxglove, balm, bedstraw, weld, woad, sweet cicely and artemisia. Brushing against many of these plants is enough to release their sweet odours.

Getting to know herbs

First you must decide the size and location of your herb garden. Most herbs need three conditions: sun, compatible soil chemistry, and good drainage—most herbs are native to the Mediterranean coast and will not grow well if their roots are constantly moist (except mints). Most, but not all, herbs are sun lovers. Chervil and tarragon will grow in partial shade; sweet woodruff grows best in shade. As for soil chemistry, most herbs prefer alkaline (or sweet) soil. Sweet woodruff is about the only herb that grows in acid soil. Soil samples can be tested by your county agricultural advisor; autumn is the best season for testing your soil.

What to grow is really a matter of personal taste, but you should know the characteristics of each herb you choose. Is it an annual, biennial, or perennial? Annuals, as the word implies, grow for one year, set seed, and die. Biennials, of which parsley is one, take two years to reach maturity, but leaves are often more flavourful the first year. (Hence parsley is often treated as an annual). Perennials continue to grow year after year, coming up each spring from the old roots.

Annual and perennial herbs make perfectly good companions in a garden; a few annuals give you a chance to vary your menus. How many plants of each variety to grow depends on how you plan to use them. You might have one rosemary plant for day-to-day cooking, for example, and one to pot as a winter house plant to grow indoors.

Consider whether the plants you want to grow can be started from seed or are better bought as seedlings from a nursery. Some must start as seedlings unless you are skilled at plant propagation. Tarragon, for example, cannot be grown from seed; and some herbs, such as rosemary and parsley grow so slowly that it seems you are waiting for ever. It is less expensive to start herbs from seed, but if you have limited time or patience, buy healthy seedlings.

Herbs, like other plants, have various growing habits. Some are sprawling, others erect. Some, like mint, spread rapidly from their roots and will take over your garden if you let them. Rather than fight the sprawling tendencies of mint, some gardeners plant it at the back of the garden, more or less out of sight and in a place where it is welcome to sprawl if it likes. (Mint comes in many flavours—spearmint, peppermint, orange mint, etc.) Some gardeners use a metal edging strip sunk around the mint bed to forestall spreading.

Also consider plant heights. Tall plants may block sunlight and air from smaller ones and are better placed along the garden's edges. There are exceptions here, too, and experience is often the best guide. You might want

"Gathering Herbs" is the title of this illustration from a 16th century herbal, the *Grete Herball*.

a single tall plant to accent a low bed; you can use angelica, a statuesque plant, that way, and crystallize its stems to decorate trifles and cakes or flavour rhubarb pie. The chart on pages 127 and 128 gives the heights the various herbs will grow to.

Easy-to-care-for herbs

It is a good idea to have a path to walk on when you harvest herbs. In the kitchen garden, pictured on page 116, the path is made of bricks. Large rocks made stepping stones in the fragrant garden.

Be sure to choose a sunny spot for your herb garden, sheltered from strong winds. Good drainage is really the most important requirement.

Herbs do not need a rich soil; in fact, with most it is better not to add fertilizer unless growth seems weak and straggly. In the spring when you plant, add a layer of mulch. This is helpful because few weeds grow through it, and it helps to retain moisture during dry spells. Add mulch once, about the middle of the growing season.

You will soon learn the particular growing requirements of each herb. Basil, for instance, comes up very quickly; people joke that when you sow basil seeds, you just stamp on them and when you turn around, they are up. With experience, you will remember the seasonal timetable of herb growing, but if you are a beginner, it is helpful to keep a journal that you can refer to each year. If you are starting herbs from seed, it is wise to plant the perennials indoors in late winter, since they take longer than annuals to come up.

A newly-planted garden should be well watered initially, but after herbs are well started, they should be kept relatively dry. Herbs repel most insects, so there is no need to spray them.

Planting seeds and seedlings

When you plant seeds, follow the instructions on the back of the packet. Mark rows so you will know what each herb is. Used wooden ice cream spoons make unobtrusive markers; write each herb's name on a spoon with waterproof ink.

A small plant, either started indoors in late winter or purchased at a nursery, is planted in the garden by tapping it out of its container and placing it in well dug soil so that the seedling is growing at the same soil level as it was in the pot. The loose soil should be firmed around the plant's soil ball so that the tender seedling is well anchored and will not be blown over by wind. Soil should be kept moist, but never soggy, until the plant is established so water well in its initial stages.

Indoor gardening

Some of the herbs that grow best indoors are those frequently used in cooking. A pot garden is a way for flat-dwellers and people who do not have gardens to have herbs at their fingertips in any season. Herbs can be placed in individual pots, or several herbs can be planted together in one large container such as the hanging basket on the next page. As with the outdoor garden, indoor herbs are easy to care for, needing mainly sun, air, water, good drainage and occasional fertilizing. Using them will automatically prune them. Indoor plants can be started from seeds or seedlings, or can be dug up from your outdoor garden and brought indoors at the end of the outdoor growing season.

For a pot herb garden use clay pots. Plant one kind of herb in each pot. A good size pot is about 10 cm in diameter, measured across the top. Use pieces of broken pot or small stones to cover the drainage hole in the bottom of the pot. Then fill pots with sterile potting soil.

If you are planting seeds, follow planting directions on the back of the packet. After planting, keep the pots out of direct sunlight until the seeds germinate and shoots appear. (The time period varies from herb to herb.) When seedlings have grown a few leaves, thin them out, leaving the three strongest well-spaced plants. The shoots you remove are flavourful and can be used in cooking at that tender age.

Water herbs when the soil feels dry, usually about every two days. Do not let the pots sit in saucers of water. Herbs will thrive on a sunny window sill or on a table where they will get daylight and fresh air.

Some herbs to grow in an indoor garden

Annuals

Basil
Ocimum basilicum

Chervil
Anthriscus cerefolium

Coriander
Coriandrum sativum

Dill
Peucedanum graveolens

Parsley
Petroselinum crispum

Summer savory
Satureia hortensis

Perennials

Chives
Allium schoenoprasum

Marjoram
Oreganum majorana

Mint
Mentha(sp)

Oregano
Origanum vulgare

Rosemary
Rosmarinus officinalis

Sage
Salvia officinalis

Tarragon
Artemisia dracunculus

Thyme
Thymus vulgaris and Thymus citriodorus

Winter savory
Satureia montana

An indoor hanging herb garden of chives, oregano, lemon thyme, marjoram, parsley, winter savory, rosemary, sage and basil has been planted in a wire basket lined with sphagnum moss. As the garden grows it fills out and trailing herbs hide most of the moss.

Greenery and Growing Things
Hanging Garden

The hanging basket of herbs in the photograph on the left is a more unusual indoor herb garden. It was planted as an experiment—to see whether the plants would yield enough to be practical. They have. You need a 30 cm wire hanging basket, 1 bag of shredded sphagnum moss and 1 bag of potting compost. These are available at garden centres and nurseries. In this hanging garden are chives, oregano, lemon thyme, marjoram, parsley, winter savory, rosemary, sage and basil, all of which were bought as small plants for this project. You could make such an indoor garden from rooted cuttings.

To make the hanging garden, soak the sphagnum moss in water (the sink is a good place to do this) then squeeze out the excess water. Line the wire basket with this moss, filling the spaces between the wires with bits of moss to hide the wire as much as possible. Fill the lined basket with potting compost. Press plants firmly into soil, allowing 3 to 5 cm of growing space.

After the basket is planted, water gently but thoroughly. The moss absorbs moisture like a sponge. Hang the basket where it will receive direct sunlight and where air can circulate freely around it. Water daily; an easy way is to throw on a few ice cubes. Every two weeks or so take the basket down and give it a good soaking in the sink or outdoors. Drain thoroughly before re-hanging. You will need to fertilize your hanging garden: use an all-purpose, water soluble fertilizer, following directions for use on the container.

The basket on the left was planted only a few weeks before the photograph was taken. As the herbs grow, they will be pinched back by taking sprigs from the ends of stems. Pinching stimulates branching and the garden will then fill out more so that the herbs hide the moss.

Greenery and Growing Things
Harvesting and Drying

Once your herbs are growing, outdoors or indoors, they can be used for flavouring and fragrance. All you need to do is harvest them. Some herbs, such as mints, are grown only for their leaves; others, like dill and fennel for seeds as well as leaves; still others for the stem, like angelica or horseradish.

Harvesting of most culinary herbs can start as soon as the plant is large enough not to miss a few leaves. Pinch off the top leaves and ends of the stems with your thumb and index finger, just as you would pinch back a house plant.

Though fresh herbs are a joy to use in cooking and many recipes call for fresh herbs, you can also dry herbs to cook with in winter and for such gifts as sachets and herb pillows and to press for note paper.

Herbs for drying can be harvested any time during the growing season. Herbs tend to lose some of their flavour during the drying process so they should be picked during the flowering period. The best time to harvest for flavour comes when the plants are just starting to bloom: that is when the aromatic oils are most concentrated in the leaves. Pick herbs in the morning, just after the dew has dried and before the sun is hot.

Herbs harvested for seeds, such as coriander and dill, should be cut when the seed heads turn brown but before they fully ripen. If you wait too long, the seeds will drop to the ground and be lost, or you will have volunteers next year. Cut the whole seed head from the stem with garden scissors.

Drying balm

In drying herbs, the objective is to remove moisture from the leaves as quickly as possible, in order to preserve the colour and flavour or fragrance. Drying time varies from herb to herb and also depends on the humidity of the air. Balm, for example, takes about a week to dry; then it can be used for tea (see page 123) or stored in an airtight container until needed for other projects.

To dry balm or any other herb, strip the leaves off the stems and spread them in a thin layer on a screen tray. Leaves should not touch one another because air must reach all of them evenly. A multi-layered tray accommodates several herbs at the same time.

One way to dry herbs is on a screen tray. The tray pictured has three tiers; you could dry rose petals on one and a different herb on each of the other two, but a single-layer tray is adequate. In fact, if you do not have a screen tray, just prop up an old window screen so that air can circulate under and over it.

Strip the leaves off the harvested stems and spread them in a single layer on the screen. Small herbs such as thyme and savory can be left on their stems for drying. After laying the leaves on the screen, keep it in a warm, dry, airy but not sunny place such as an attic. When one side is dry—with balm after three days—turn the leaves and let the other side dry. Drying herbs usually takes a week or less. The time is shortened in dry weather. If you dry herbs outside, bring them inside each evening so dew will not dampen them.

The leaves are dry when they are crisp, and then it is time to remove them from the screen tray. Seed heads are dried in the same way as leaves.

Another method of drying suitable for herbs with long stems such as marjoram, sage, mint, and rosemary is to fasten the stems together in a bunch with a rubber band and hang them in a warm, dry, airy place. They are decorative in a country kitchen. Many people hang bunches upside down and may even put them in paper bags to keep light from discolouring the leaves, but herbs dry just as well right side up, and make a pretty bouquet. Check the bunches every two days or so until you find the leaves are crackly dry.

Storing

When herbs on the screen tray or hanging in bunches are dry, you will need to store them if you are not using them right away. Many people use jars and bottles to store herbs, but they will lose flavour or fragrance if kept this way for any length of time, unless the containers have airtight stoppers. As soon as herbs are dry, remove the leaves from the stems and pack leaves in airtight containers or plastic bags. Whole leaves are better than those that are broken or crumbled because they keep their flavour longer. Store seeds, too, in airtight containers. Keep all dried herbs in a dark, cool place. Tarragon, chives, and parsley can be preserved by freezing. Cut herb tips in the morning, wash them and pat them dry. Freeze small amounts in tightly-sealed plastic bags. You will soon learn the amount you usually use in a recipe, so none will be wasted. (Frozen herbs should not be re-frozen.)

Herb tea or tisane

Balm is one of the many herbs that can be used to make a tasty tea. Others are lemon verbena, mint, rosemary, sage, and thyme; in fact, almost any of the culinary herbs can be used. A heaped teaspoon of the dried herb is needed for each cup of boiling water. Fresh herbs can also be used, but use about 2 heaped teaspoons of fresh leaves per cup. To make herb tea, put the herbs in a warm teapot and add boiling water. Let the mixture steep for 10 minutes. It will be light-coloured. If you want a stronger flavour, add more of the herb. Never use milk, but do use honey to sweeten.

Introduce a friend to herb gardening with this tiny flower basket of thyme, lavender, marjoram, and other herbs. The herbs can root in potting compost. Flowers include geraniums and heartsease.

Greenery and Growing Things
Gift Basket

A good way to get a friend started as a herb gardener is to give a basket of living herbs. You can make such baskets for friends who are ill, for presents or special occasions, using whatever fresh herbs are available at the moment. The rooting soil is a potting compost that is good to have on hand all the time for numerous gardening needs.

You can use miniature baskets available in gift or novelty shops. The basket can be any size—those 5 to 8 cm square work well. In addition to the basket and herbs, you need a container or containers to hold the soil—or florist's Oasis, if you do not want to root the herbs; paper cups will do, or small plastic containers such as individual ice cube holders, or you can make a liner of aluminium foil with joints tightly creased. The basket liner should be trimmed if necessary, so that it does not show over the top of the basket.

The day before you want to assemble the basket, use a sharp knife to cut herbs 8 to 10 cm long, making the cut at an angle just below a leaf or leaf node. Put cuttings in a glass of water overnight so they will be turgid when you are ready to place them in the soil.

To assemble the basket, fill the container with soil mix and wet it. Arrange the plants in an attractive way in the basket (see photograph on the left). Another method is first to dip the ends of the herbs in hormone rooting powder, available at plant shops, and then insert them in the soil.

The basket is then ready to present. Culinary herbs that will root easily are thyme, marjoram, oregano, lavender, and rosemary, savory, mints and geraniums. But you can use any herb for such a basket according to what you have available, and what you think the person will appreciate.

Designs and Decorations
Herb Note Cards

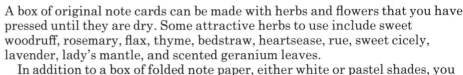

A box of original note cards can be made with herbs and flowers that you have pressed until they are dry. Some attractive herbs to use include sweet woodruff, rosemary, flax, thyme, bedstraw, heartsease, rue, sweet cicely, lavender, lady's mantle, and scented geranium leaves.

In addition to a box of folded note paper, either white or pastel shades, you will need: sheets of Japanese rice paper cut the same size as the note card front or slightly larger (rice paper is available at craft shops); box of wallpaper paste; and a sponge. If you wish to spray the note cards to show silhouettes of leaves as in the bottom card in the photograph on the left, you will also need a can of green spray paint.

First make the paste by mixing 3 tablespoons of wallpaper paste with 500 ml of water. Then apply the paste evenly to a note card front, using a sponge or soft brush. Arrange the pressed herb or herbs to your liking. It is best to use only one or two pressed leaves per card to avoid a cluttered look.

Carefully place a piece of rice paper over the arranged herbs and wet with more of the paste solution. Use a sponge and be careful to eliminate any air bubbles so that the rice paper lies flat. While it is wet, trim any extra rice paper from the edges with your thumb and index finger or with scissors.

Let the card dry and begin working on the next card. When dry, it may be necessary to press the card back lightly with a warm (not hot) iron for a flatter look. It is fine, however, to leave cards looking slightly irregular.

Additional dried leaves can be silhouetted with spray paint to produce a shadow effect. If you wish to do this, place a leaf on top of the rice paper where you want the leaf impression, and carefully spray over the leaf. When you remove the leaf, its silhouette will show in white.

The card is finished, and when dry the message can be written inside.

Blank note cards decorated with pressed herbs include blue flax (top card) and rosemary and heartsease (bottom).

Tarragon mixed with a savoury filling makes delicious hors d'oeuvres. Here white bread is carefully rolled to encase filling before baking. Baked rolls sit in bowl on the right.

Kitchen Favourites and Celebrations
Herbs in the Kitchen

Herbs transform many run-of-the-mill recipes into unusual and tempting fare. A few, simple "rules of herbal thumb" are all you need to get started with cooking with herbs. First, use herbs sparingly; they should accent, not disguise, the flavour of the food. Second, for a recipe serving four, start with $\frac{1}{4}$ teaspoon powdered, $\frac{1}{2}$ teaspoon dried, or 1 tablespoon of a fresh herb. Finally, try herbs with old stand-by recipes in the beginning. For example, you might prepare a chicken the way you normally do, but add an accent of rosemary and see if your family likes it. This is especially effective if you have young children who are reluctant to try new foods.

Herbs can make a fine substitute for a basting brush, especially at barbecues. Pick a small bunch of herbs—rosemary, lovage, oregano, savory, mint, or marjoram—and use the herbs to brush the marinade on the meat as it cooks. A simple marinade of lemon juice and olive oil is suitable for most types of meat including fish.

Cook's guide to herbs

Soups:
Basil, bay, chives, dill, oregano, parsley, tarragon

Eggs:
Basil, coriander, cress, dill, parsley, tarragon, thyme

Breads:
Caraway, chives, dill, garlic, marjoram, parsley, rosemary, tarragon

Fish:
Chives, dill, fennel, parsley, tarragon, chervil, basil

Meats:
Basil, dill, marjoram, mint, oregano, rosemary, sage, summer savory, thyme

Poultry:
Basil, dill, balm, lovage, sage, tarragon, thyme

Salad and salad dressings:
Basil, chives, cress, dill, garlic, marjoram, oregano, parsley, savory, tarragon

Drinks:
Dandelion, balm, lemon verbena, mint, sweet woodruff

Tarragon Savoury Rolls

These excellent hors d'oeuvres (shown on the previous page) may be frozen and simply baked when friends drop in unexpectedly.

1½ tablespoons chopped shallots
1 tablespoon butter
1 tablespoon chopped fresh
   tarragon
   (or ½ teaspoon dried tarragon)
2 tablespoons flour

500 g minced clams: or cooked chicken
   tuna fish, or mushrooms
¼ teaspoon Worcestershire sauce
pinch of mace
14 slices white bread with crusts
   removed
55 g butter

To make filling: Sauté shallots and tarragon in 1 tablespoon butter in a frying-pan. Blend in flour, Worcestershire sauce and mace. Add clams and liquid (or alternative filling) and cook slowly over medium heat until thick. Cool.

Melt butter over low heat. Flatten each slice of white bread with a rolling-pin until thin. Brush with melted butter and spread with a small amount (about 1 tablespoon) of the clam mixture. Roll the bread tightly (see photograph on previous page) and cut each roll into three sections. Brush the tops with melted butter and sprinkle each with a dash of paprika.

Bake on baking sheets for 10 minutes at 220° C, mark 7, and serve. If the clam rolls were frozen, bake for 15 minutes at the same temperature.

Pesto Sauce for pasta

This recipe specifies equal amounts of fresh basil and parsley, though some versions just call for basil. It is also possible to make pesto with dill or marjoram. Pesto sauce can be put in jars and refrigerated or deep-frozen. If you plan to refrigerate it for any length of time, spread a few drops of oil on the top of the sauce, to prevent mould. This recipe makes about 300 ml.

230 ml oil (olive oil, corn oil or 115 ml of each,
well mixed)
45 g firmly packed fresh basil, or 15 g dried basil
30 g firmly packed fresh parsley

4 small cloves garlic
115 g pine nuts or walnuts
½ teaspoon salt
pinch black pepper

If you have a blender, simply blend all ingredients until smooth. Store in a refrigerator, but let stand at room temperature for ½ hour before serving.

To make pesto by hand, crush the coarsely chopped fresh parsley and fresh or dried basil with a mortar and pestle, or place in a heavy mixing bowl and crush with a wooden spoon, until herbs are smooth and almost pastelike. Mix in the salt, pepper, garlic and nuts; add half the oil, and continue to crush the herbs while working in the remainder of the oil.

To serve four people: Prepare 500 g of fettucini (or other pasta) according to package directions. While pasta is cooking, saute 115 g of mushrooms in butter. Drain pasta and put in serving dish. Top with mushrooms and 4 tablespoons of the sauce. Mix well, and serve with grated Parmesan cheese.

Mint Syrup

Fresh mint leaves can be used in a surprising array of recipes, including this unusual mint syrup which can be used in juleps, as a sweetener for punch, or to flavour iced or hot tea. Several varieties of mint can be used to make the syrup: apple, spearmint, orange mint and peppermint, but the syrup can be made of spearmint alone. This recipe makes about 1 litre of mint syrup.
Preparation: Strip and pack 3 cupfuls of fresh mint leaves. Squeeze 1 cup of lemon juice (seeds and pulp, too) and save the rind from 3 lemons. Squeeze 1 cup of orange juice, including seeds and pulp. Save rind from 1 orange.

Boil 3 cups of water with 2 cups of sugar for 3 minutes. Add the lemon juice and rind and boil 3 minutes more. Add the orange juice and rind and boil for another three minutes. Add mint leaves; boil 3 minutes more. Pour mixture through a colander or strainer, mashing well with a wooden spoon. Cool.

A pesto sauce of basil and parsley enhances any pasta. Here it is used with fettucini, graciously served in a pewter dish and accompanied by a separate bowl of grated cheese.

Pointed-leaved spearmint and round-leaved apple mint are two varieties that can be combined for mint syrup, a drink sweetener.

Mint juleps with a tang are made by pouring 1 part of mint syrup and 1 part of bourbon over crushed ice. Garnish with fresh mint.

Popular and useful herbs

These herbs are arranged according to their common names. On the right of each herb's illustration is its botanical name, description, and useful growing information.

Balm

Melissa officinalis
Perennial
Uses: culinary, fragrance

Crinkly green leaves about 5 to 8 cm long with scalloped borders. Plant grows 30 to 60 cm tall and bears tiny, bushy, white flowers during summer.

Strong lemon-scented leaves. Flourishes in full sun or partial shade, and has a tendency to spread. Use leaves from early spring to late autumn.

Basil, sweet

Ocimum basilicum
Annual
Use: culinary

Light green plant that grows 30 to 60 cm tall. Small, shiny leaves 2.5 to 5 cm long. Small white flowers grow in spikes at the ends of the stems.

Grows in full sun and seed is quick to germinate. Green leaves can be picked after approximately 6 weeks. Bush basil is a decorative variety that is more insect-free.

Burnet, salad

Sanguisorba minor
Perennial
Use: culinary

Bushy plant 30 to 60 cm tall bearing feathery, fern-like notched leaves. Grows in clumps. Rose-coloured flowers top tall stems arising from the centre of the bush.

Grows well in sunlight in well-drained soil. Easy to start from seed. Tastes like cucumber. Add fresh leaves to salads, drinks, and cheese. Cutting off flower stems encourages leaf growth.

Chives

Allium schoenoprasum
Perennial
Use: culinary

Hollow, onion-like leaves growing in clumps that reach about 25 cm in height. Clusters of lavender flowers appear just above the leaves in spring.

Grows in sun. Usually bought as small plants but can be started from seeds though this takes about a year to yield usable plants. Delicate onion-like flavour; used fresh or frozen to season many dishes.

Dill

Peucedanum graveolens
Annual
Use: culinary

Grows about 1 metre tall. Feathery light green, many-branched leaves grow on blue-green stems. In mid-summer, yellow flowers appear and ripen into small brown seeds.

Cultivated for the pungent flavour of seeds; used for making pickles, and in a variety of other recipes. Grows quickly in full sun. Seeds should be planted in spring. Harvest the entire plant in early autumn or seeds will self-sow.

Garlic

Allium sativum
Perennial
Use: culinary

Grows from bulbs that break into small sections called cloves; flat narrow leaves grow approximately 60 cm long and are topped by globes of white flowers.

Bulb multiplies into 8 to 12 cloves during the growing season. These are dug up for use and re-planting. Harvest when leaves die after flowering.

Marjoram, sweet

Origanum majorana
Perennial
Use: culinary

Low, spreading, bushy plant some 20 to 30 cm high. Velvety, oval, grey-green leaves; small white flowers grow from knot-like leaf clusters at the end of stems.

Easily grown from seeds in spring. Cutting off the leafy stems stimulates growth of new stems and leaves. Treat as a pot plant during winter.

Mint

Mentha (sp)
Perennial
Uses: culinary, fragrance

Growth varies with species, from 30 to 90 cm. Most common is spearmint which has crisp, dark green crinkly leaves about 5 cm long. Plant grows 30 to 60 cm tall and spreads rampantly.

Cultivated for scented leaves. Will grow in sun or partial shade. Spreads rapidly by means of underground stems. Leaves can be picked any time, stimulating new growth.

Savory, summer

Satureia hortensia
Annual
Use: culinary

Narrow, dark green leaves, upright stems, often branching; 30 to 60 cm tall. Pink flowers appear about 2 months after sowing.

Grows in full sun. Leaves can be picked any time for fresh use. Delicate pepper flavour. Used with meats and vegetables.

Oregano

Origanum vulgare
Perennial
Use: culinary

Grows 60 to 75 cm tall; grey-green oval leaves that come to a blunt point. White, pink and purple flowers.

Also known as wild marjoram. Grows in sun and spreads rapidly. Flowers should be cut back. Makes a good container plant. Use fresh leaves or dried.

Savory, winter

Satureia montana
Perennial
Use: culinary

Lower, more spreading growth than summer savory. Dark green, shiny leaves. Grows 30 to 60 cm tall with light green stems at the upper ends of a woody base.

A good border plant; woody stems should be trimmed back to 10 cm in spring. Dried leaves excellent with beans and eggs.

Parsley

Petroselinum crispum
Biennial treated as an annual
Use: culinary

Grows about 30 cm tall in clumps. Curly parsley, the most popular species, has bright green serrated edges and crinkled leaves. Italian parsley has coarse flat leaves, but has more flavour.

Slow to germinate; most gardeners prefer to put in new plants each spring. Grows best in full sun.

Tarragon (French)

Artemisia dracunculus
Perennial
Use: culinary

Thin bush with 3 cm long slender green leaves; grows 30 to 75 cm tall.

Needs well-drained soil and full or partial sun. Will not produce seeds; grows from cuttings or divisions. Should not be confused with Russian tarragon which does seed. Can be used to flavour vinegar.

Rosemary

Rosmarinus officinalis
Perennial
Use: culinary

Evergreen shrub with needle-like leaves that grows 60 to 90 cm tall. Produces blue-purple flowers.

Needs full sun and grows best in soil containing lime. In cold climates, it is brought indoors in winter. Leaves have a pine-like aroma and are especially good with meats.

Thyme

Thymus vulgaris
Perennial
Use: culinary

Small bush 15 to 30 cm tall; can spread 45 cm or more. Tiny, oval, evergreen leaves and small purple flowers.

Grows in well-drained soil that is fairly dry. Used sparingly as it has a strong flavour. Attracts bees.